Demobilizing Irregular Forces

For Karen and Erin

Demobilizing Irregular Forces

Eric Y. Shibuya

polity

First published in 2012 by Polity Press

Polity Press
65 Bridge Street
Cambridge CB2 1UR, UK

Polity Press
350 Main Street
Malden, MA 02148, USA

ISBN-13: 978-0-7456-4885-9 (hardback)
ISBN-13: 978-0-7456-4886-6 (paperback)

A catalogue record for this book is available from the British Library.

Typeset in 10.25 on 13 pt Scala
by Servis Filmsetting Ltd, Stockport, Cheshire
Printed and bound in Great Britain by MPG Books Group Limited, Bodmin, Cornwall

The publisher has used its best endeavours to ensure that the URLs for external websites referred to in this book are correct and active at the time of going to press. However, the publisher has no responsibility for the websites and can make no guarantee that a site will remain live or that the content is or will remain appropriate.

Every effort has been made to trace all copyright holders, but if any have been inadvertently overlooked the publisher will be pleased to include any necessary credits in any subsequent reprint or edition.

For further information on Polity, visit our website: www.politybooks.com

Contents

Acknowledgements

My sincere thanks to Louise Knight and David Winters at Polity Books for taking a chance on a first-time book writer, and for their understanding for the delays incurred when "real life" intruded onto my writing time. Clare Ansell and Susan Beer put the book together beautifully. I would also acknowledge the two anonymous reviewers whose comments improved this work. All errors and omissions, of course, are mine alone.

I owe a great deal to good mentors. Richard Chadwick at the University of Hawaii, Stephen Sloan at the University of Oklahoma, and Dimitris Stevis and Sue Ellen Charlton at Colorado State University. In my career, I have been blessed with supportive colleagues and engaged students. First at the Asia-Pacific Center for Security Studies and now at Marine Corps University, the men and women I have worked with have been some of the most dedicated leaders and educators I have had the pleasure of working with. I could easily name them all, but special mention goes to Chris Jasparro, Terry Klapakis, and Paul Smith, as well as Willy Buhl, Rich DiNardo, Paul Gelpi, John Karagosian, Frank Marlo, Doug McKenna, BJ Payne, Paul Pond, Erin Simpson, and Brian Yee. As for my students, I thank you for your service and for all of our discussions, which either sharpened my arguments and thinking or simply made me laugh (intentionally or otherwise) when I needed it.

Finally and most importantly, this book is dedicated to my

wife Karen and our daughter Erin. They are the center of my world and I thank them for their understanding when this book inevitably pulled me away from "family time." Thank you, I love you both. Now, let's go play.

CHAPTER ONE

Introduction

The early stages of the conflicts in Afghanistan and Iraq in 2002 and 2003 respectively only served to confirm what most analysts had concluded from Operation Desert Storm nearly a decade prior. Simply put, modern militaries (most especially the United States) had become so effective at waging conventional warfare that engaging them in such a manner would place most adversaries at a great disadvantage. Indeed, such concerns were expressed even before Afghanistan and Iraq.[1] However, while a great deal of attention focused on the effectiveness of the United States and other modern militaries in waging and winning wars, there was a growing, parallel analysis suggesting that this greater effectiveness had not extended to the post-conflict situation. "Winning wars" was one thing, but "securing the peace" another matter entirely. Modern militaries had focused on the obvious dangers of warfighting, while post-conflict "stabilization" measures were often seen as someone else's problem (this despite the long history of the military role in post-conflict stabilization).

While the end of the Cold War gave greater freedom of action to Western nations, international organizations such as the United Nations, and regional organizations as well (African Union, Pacific Islands Forum, etc.), the removal of the Cold War context revealed the greater complexity underlying much of these "new" conflicts. Third-party interventions could "do" more, but that did not mean they knew how to help. In fact, this ability to intervene "sooner" than in the past is further complicated by not simply the post Cold War context, but rather by the post World War II "norm" that military conquest will no longer be an acceptable way of gaining territory. Hence, military interventions today seek to stabilize post-conflict environments without "occupying" them in the political sense. This creates the paradoxical situation of an international coalition expressing commitment to spend the time and resources to assist in stabilizing a region after conflict, but also promising to leave as soon as possible.

Civil Conflict and its Aftermath

The challenge of an armed group is one of the most critical issues any state can face. Its veneer of legitimacy in jeopardy, a government must find ways to lower levels of violence and either punish the perpetrators or answer their grievances. In either case, the government must also address any passive support for the group and bring those individuals back into the fold. However, the rise of an armed force is only a symptom of a much deeper issue – the deep insecurity and lack of faith the population has in the state apparatus. This insecurity arises from two main situations. In the first case, the government security structure cannot provide for basic security from unacceptable levels of targeted violence. Phil Williams discusses this situation in post-2003 Iraq. Williams argues, "[the armed groups] originated or (where they already existed) expanded largely because of the inability of the [Coalition Provisional Authority] and subsequently the Iraqi Government to provide security to Iraq's Shiite majority."[2] In the second case, the government security forces are *themselves* the source of threat to the community. In either situation, the government's lack of ability or inclination to provide basic security is a major motivating factor in the creation and evolution of armed groups from outside the government system.

The end of the Cold War allowed for greater intervention by the international community to preserve global stability. These increasing interventions have led to an ironic situation of chronic *tensions*, if not *conflict*. Decisive conclusions to conflicts have become increasingly rare in the modern world. It is no longer acceptable, for the most part, to take territory from another country after victory in conflict. The international community either through regional or international organizations and/or coalitions has, especially in the post Cold War world, inserted itself between warring parties in an effort to bring an end to the violence. These operations hope to create "breathing space" between opposing parties in an effort to diffuse tensions, and to create the initial conditions for a peaceful society. The end of chronic organized armed violence does not lead automatically to peace; indeed, it is frequently the case that the end of "organized" or "political" violence leads simply to disorganized violence and/or criminal banditry.[3] Whatever the term, it is certainly not "peace." Third parties and outsiders can certainly contribute, but fundamentally, peace must be cultivated from *within* a society. The international community generally recognizes their contribution to developing this peace as having three major elements: the physical removal and/or destruction of much of the weaponry in the area, the elimination of the (quasi-) military or security force structures, and finally a process whereby former combatants are brought into the rest of the community. These respective processes comprise the Disarmament, Demobilization, and Reintegration (DDR) program.

Organization of the Book

This book does not intend to set out uniform "guidelines" for DDR. In fact, one of the central premises of this book is that the situations and background context of any case are too varied to suggest a universal blueprint for DDR that will work in all cases. While there are of course many valuable lessons taken from each case, this does not (and should not) establish a DDR "doctrine." Certainly, in the United States, there is a mental bias for just such a blueprint in areas of military planning. The most recent example being the development of the counterinsurgency (COIN) manual based on the initial experiences of the wars in Iraq and Afghanistan.[4] Many scholars in the counterinsurgency field would characterize the manual as "old wine in new wineskin,"[5] and indeed the COIN manual does draw from some of the classic works in the counterinsurgency literature.[6] Other critics put forward the more operational concern that the emphasis placed on counterinsurgency will cripple the American military's abilities to deal with more conventional threats.[7] Both criticisms are not without merit, but are beyond the scope of this book. The COIN manual is noted here as an object lesson. While the manual establishes a "doctrine" of counterinsurgency, doctrine should not be dogma.

Perhaps even more important than "how" an action (be it COIN, DDR, or some other "nonconventional" military operation) is conducted is the question of "who" conducts (or at the very least, leads) them. There are serious considerations of "insider/outsider" issues that impact the ability of parties to intervene effectively. While most of the general precepts are the same for DDR no matter who leads the program, some differences between internal government and foreign government (or international agencies) interventions do exist, especially in terms of what practices are deemed to be culturally acceptable. This is especially true for operations such as COIN and DDR where there is great potential for the use of violence. Patrick Bishop, writing about the experiences of British paratroopers in Afghanistan, discusses an attempt to bring the tribal elders together for a meeting. Rather than voluntary attendance, the Afghan National Army forces all of the elders to attend. While the practice was heavy-handed, Bishop notes that this actually protected the elders from the Taliban, as the elders could claim that they were coerced to attend. Bishop says, "It was the Afghan way of doing things. But it was not an example that the rules the British imposed on themselves allowed them to follow."[8] What Bishop misses in his criticism is that these "rules" are not a limitation, but a byproduct of the recognition that the British *cannot* act in the same fashion as the Afghan soldiers because they lack the cultural legitimacy to do so. Just as in COIN operations, the cultural norms of the affected populations must be taken into account as the DDR program is implemented.

The deeper question for understanding and evaluating the impact of "Insiders" vs. "Outsiders" in DDR projects is whether similar phenomena are manifesting due to the same causes or whether different underlying dynamics are appearing in similar ways. Whoever the initiating agent is, the purpose of DDR remains the same: DDR programs must contribute to the longer-term goal of establishing a solid post-conflict peace. (This is not the same as saying that DDR must establish a solid post-conflict peace, although this distinction is not always clear.) This book aims to focus thematically on the various phases of the DDR program, rather than (as is usually the case in the academic literature) an analysis of the DDR process within a single case.

The next chapter provides a brief overview of the history and evolution of the DDR enterprise. There are some interesting lessons provided by earlier DDR cases, but the major growth in the DDR enterprise occurs in the post Cold War era, as the end of the bipolar conflict gives the international community (particularly international organizations like the United Nations and World Bank) greater freedom to maneuver. However, this subsequent increase in "peacekeeping" operations (an obvious misnomer in many cases, as there was at best only an illusion of peace in some cases) and other military interventions may have had the inadvertent consequence of ending conflict for the time being, but not alleviating the tensions between the competing parties. A group that considers "victory" as being stolen from them due to intervention may hope to continue the conflict when the intervention force leaves, and DDR is part of the process to prevent such actions from "spoilers."

The DDR process is best considered as a symbiotic, holistic process. However, there is some analytical clarity to be gained by focusing on each part of the DDR process in isolation. The following chapters will therefore consider each component of the DDR process separately, keeping in mind the critical requirement of integrating (or more likely, understanding their points of reinforcement) DDR in practice. The next chapter will discuss the disarmament phase of DDR. It considers the various facets that go into an effective disarmament program and discusses how and why the international community in general has seemed preoccupied with this particular dimension of DDR to the detriment of the wider goal of initiating the building of a sustainable post-conflict peace environment. The great visibility of the disarmament phase is very attractive to political leaders (who can point to the program as evidence that "something is being done") but this activity may have little to do in the end with setting the conditions for a long-term peace.

The next chapter focuses on the demobilization phase of the process. While disarmament reduces the possibility that minor grievances can quickly escalate into acts of major violence, the demobilization phase is where the process of peacebuilding moves from simply the absence of organized, politically oriented violence towards stabilization and the beginnings of reconciliation. The more obvious manifestations of demobilization are when combatants surrender uniforms and insignia (if they exist), and no longer view themselves as part of a larger military unit. The less obvious but more significant aspect of the demobilization process is the psychological shift wherein the former combatants leave the context and structures of their fighting groups and begin to enter civilian life. The duration of the conflict and (more individually) the length of time the combatant was engaged, directly or indirectly, in conflict can have somewhat contradictory effects on the ease of demobilization. Combatants who have been in combat for much of their lives may find it very difficult to leave that structure and reinsert themselves into the larger society. For many, the resistance toward demobilization and reintegration may have less to do with the desire for peace than with the fear of uncertainty. This is especially true of child soldiers, who have had little or no connection to a non-combat lifestyle. However, in other cases the overall duration of the conflict can strengthen and empower the communal desire to end the violence, a phenomenon referred to as "war fatigue."

Perhaps most important to consider, while the disarmament phase is most often led primarily by the military, it is during the demobilization phase that the handover of control and responsibility usually shifts from the military to civilian-led agencies and organizations. This aspect has been mentioned in the literature, but considerations of the issues involved in this handover have not received the attention it probably deserves. This shift is not symbolic; it can entail a shift in resources, not to mention the potential bureaucratic confusion and clash of institutional cultures. Making this transition as seamless as possible requires people in different agencies to work together and to get to know and understand each other and their respective agencies, their mandates, and their capabilities.

Reintegration is undoubtedly the key aspect of the DDR

process. Effective disarmament and demobilization are only symptoms or evidence of movement towards communal reconciliation. Demobilization only works if the combatants and the larger community find themselves in positions they consider "safe." Reintegration, as the most difficult and important part of DDR, implies that there is a society, a community, for the former combatants to be brought back into. That society is often assumed to be some variation of the *status quo ante*, but if such were the case, then there would arguably have been no armed group to begin with. Reintegration is not necessarily about the previous society, but about creating an atmosphere and/or process where disagreements and grievances are addressed without violence or the chronic threat of violence. "Success" in DDR therefore takes place within the larger context of post-conflict reconciliation. Berdal notes concisely, "in the absence of political trust and a basic willingness to abide by agreements already entered into, demobilisation programmes are likely to fail, however well they are designed and financed."[9] This reconciliation is more than simply national legislation or international agreements, but perhaps even more significantly must occur at the community level. While state-to-state relations and programs may handle reconciliation at the macrolevel, community-level programs may be more important to the individuals at the grassroots, though these programs often do not get the visibility or the associated funding of national or international programs.

Successful reintegration programs are not simply "jobs programs." Specifically, they cannot be instituted as "entitlements" to ex-combatants or seen as rewards for participating in acts of violence. The violence cannot be legitimized in that fashion. Reintegration is therefore not just about bringing the combatant back into society, but also about creating a reinforcing relationship that gives the larger society the motivation to accept the combatant. Incentives for reintegration cannot be rewards for past action, but investments for future behavior.

Economic incentives and employment programs address the more physical side of reintegration. The psychological impacts must also be addressed for reintegration to work. In terms of reconciliation as a cultural practice, many societies have traditional mechanisms that contribute to building community forgiveness. These practices are usually some variation of public announcements of wrongdoing and a call to be reaccepted into the larger society. In many cultures, women play a particularly important role in these reconciliation ceremonies, and to ignore their role and status would be a significant mistake.

In some cases, modern resources (currency, in particular) have become part of these symbolic reconciliation rituals. This can have the unfortunate effect of corrupting much of the psychological value of these practices. Rather than expressions of apology and presentations of objects of symbolic value, the introduction of currency into forgiveness practices brings about an unfortunate commodification of life and death. Where these cultural practices have power, they should be encouraged; and in societies where such traditional ceremonies no longer have contemporary value, they should be carefully monitored, if not rejected outright. "Hollow" ceremonial practices are even less valuable than no reconciliation ceremony at all.

The final chapter will look at the continuing challenges for successful DDR programs. In terms of DDR, it is not that the problems are hard to identify; it is that they are so hard to solve. Should the focus of the DDR program be on establishing security, or a larger focus on development? The UN Integrated DDR Standards (IDDRS) argues that the major problem in successfully implementing DDR remains the lack of integration of all facets of DDR, but can in fact DDR be more effective by focusing on security issues rather than larger development problems that are outside the expertise of security forces? Can DDR agencies achieve integration in thought while focusing on specific phases in practice? How should a DDR program overcome the tendency to bias short-term projects and overemphasize funding and effort toward them (particularly weapons collection) while failing to see the possible consequences that these efforts may have for demobilization and reintegration considerations? Efforts to include "culturally sensitive" practices of forgiveness and reconciliation are good ideas, but in some cases have failed in application. This does not mean such traditional practices should be dismissed. The DDR process can only succeed if it is understood as the *foundation* of long-term reconciliation and it is in that fashion that efforts should be focused.

The final chapter will conclude with a short reassessment of each aspect of the DDR project and the challenges in connecting them together. How to develop a DDR process where each aspect does in fact reinforce the others, and the entire project is focused on a long-term peace, is the ultimate goal of any DDR project. While the international community today practically takes for granted the need for a DDR program in any post-conflict situation, there is a lack of evidence that DDR is in fact tied to establishing peace. In one sense, this is more about overestimating what in fact a DDR program is supposed to do, but on the other hand it also suggests the need to develop better measures of effectiveness. The power and value of DDR may not be in what it does at all, but rather in what the people believe it does. DDR provides that critical "breathing space" early in the post-conflict environment, when tensions are high and trust is lacking. If DDR provides for that brief moment of calm in that moment, that may be its greatest contribution. Taking advantage of that moment and moving further towards sustainable peace may best be considered beyond the domain of "official" DDR.

CHAPTER TWO

The History and Evolution of DDR

Disarmament and Demobilization have long been an obvious occurrence of war termination. One of the most comprehensive demobilization programs in the aftermath of a major war was the post World War II occupation of Germany and Japan. As Iklé notes, the goal was not simply to remove the military capability of Germany and Japan, but to shape their societies (as well as the international context) so that these nations would no longer *want* to wage war.[1] Indeed, if one is successful in mitigating a state's *intentions* of using military means to secure its interests, then one is generally less concerned with that state's capabilities. Reintegration programs also have a long history. They are especially necessary in areas of internal conflict, to bring former fighters back into a peacetime society. In many cases, the term "reintegration" is a misnomer, as the former fighters were not ever "integrated" in the first place. (Writers of a more postmodern inclination would perhaps press the point by noting typographically the (re)integration of ex-combatants.) DDR has generally therefore been implemented in two kinds of situations: demilitarization of a defeated military force, or a war-to-peace transition in a context short of actual victory by one side.[2] In the post Cold War context, the great majority of DDR cases have been the latter type.

Antecedent cases notwithstanding, formal DDR programs run by and with the international community have really been an aspect of the post Cold War world. The "peace dividend" many expected with the end of the bipolar world system did not develop. Indeed, without the overarching threat of nuclear conflict between the superpowers, many of the underlying schisms within and between nations were now able to break out into violence. In other cases, many "proxy" wars supported during the Cold War simply continued. Hubris allowed the superpowers to consider these conflicts as minor events, and the states involved no more than pawns on the geopolitical chessboard with no will or motivations of their own. No matter how "hot" these conflicts may have been, they would surely end with the removal of external support. This of course did not happen, and in some cases, the lack of a "patron" state actually resulted in an increase in violence. The armed group may have lost its source of funding and materiel, but it is also released from any moderating influence that the patron may have had on its behavior.

While the end of the Cold War may have created the opening for the conflicts to explode, the overarching norms drawn from the end of World War II meant that even military victory would not lead to territorial conquest. The removal of the constraints of the bipolar system also created opportunities for third-party intervention (the United States, regional powers, international organizations or some combination thereof) to curtail the violence. The international community in the form of the United Nations (UN) has increasingly led these interventions. The growth and development of this kind of "peacekeeping" operation has led to greater practice and scholarship on the various aspects of DDR, and efforts to identify errors and best practices from this experience has been increasing since the late 1990s. According to Hazen, there have been over two dozen DDR projects in the last two decades, although differences in categorization and definition make an exact number difficult.[3] As of October 2011, the UN DDR Resource Center listed thirteen countries under their "country programmes" with ongoing DDR activities.[4]

The United Nations Department of Peacekeeping Operations (DPKO) published a set of principles and guidelines for DDR in December 1999. Although disarmament is usually assumed to be the first step in the process, a "Field and Classroom Guide" for DDR points out insightfully that "DDR programmes do not commence with disarmament, even though the acronym suggests [a] procedural order."[5] The experiences and lessons learned from the various DDR missions of the 1990s and into the twenty-first century gave increasing focus on the need to consider DDR more holistically. This led to the publication of the IDDRS by the UN in 2006. The IDDRS offers great insight into the DDR process and includes the experiences from a great number of cases and practitioners. However, the IDDRS document itself is symbolic of the massive problems that confront any attempt to approach DDR comprehensively and in an integrated fashion. The full document runs nearly 800 pages. A more manageable "Operational Guide" to IDDRS is available (both documents are available online), but even the Guide is over 200 pages. It is not without some irony that a guide for "integrating" the various aspects of a DDR program is actually set up for downloading in separate components for the field worker to implement. As of October 2009, there was no "easy" way to download the entire Operational Guide at once directly from the UN website (although the entire IDDRS can be downloaded with a single click).

Terminology

One issue for any study of armed groups is the problem of terminology. Is there an all-encompassing term that accurately covers the various groups under consideration? The groups themselves offer no help for the scholar/analyst. Recognizing that the fundamental nature of the struggle is political, armed groups attempt to gather whatever prestige or legitimacy they can. They use a variety of titles, calling themselves "armies," "patriotic/popular fronts," "self-defense forces," "militias," and other variations on the theme. While it is understandable for groups to use these terms for political advantage, they do not necessarily aid in achieving greater analytical clarity. One example is the use of the term "militia."

The term "militia" originally designated a civilian force raised to assist the state in times of need. This "first-generation"[6] type of militia is encapsulated in several liberal democratic constitutions. The central premise of first-generation militias is that the militia owes some kind of loyalty to the government. How much loyalty, especially regarding how much control the government has over the militia's actions, can be a significant source of tension in many cases. Some militia groups established by the state (such as in Colombia or pro-Indonesian militias in East Timor) may over time break away from government control due to disagreements over policy or approach. Some militia groups may even view themselves as preceding the state, or drawing on values or titles that helped to establish the state. The vigilante organization that patrols the border between the United States and Mexico calls itself the "Minutemen" for this reason.[7] In some cases, governments have attempted to take advantage of older, more traditional practices of security/community policing in the establishment of militia groups. Understanding a militia's identity as incorporating some loyalty to the government biases the concept of a "militia" in the direction of liberal democratic states, where the separation of state and government is less significant than in authoritarian regimes. However, if one does not connect a militia's identity with support of a government, then the term becomes more amorphous and less helpful analytically. Alden, Thakur, and Arnold attempt to conceptualize militias "as a military force composed of civilians outside of a state's formal military structure."[8] While this still can imply a connection in support of the state, they further note that "the key point of militias is that they apply violence in pursuit of their respective objectives, including *both* challenging established state power structures and acting in the interests of particular identities, including those of a state."[9] By this understanding, a "militia" does not have to *support* a state, so long as the militia understands its identity as one of "self-defense." Alden, Thakur, and Arnold, then, essentially trust the group's self-identification as a "self-defense" group to define it as a militia. Francis describes these armed groups as "second-generation" militias to separate them from earlier understandings, but while these groups may consider themselves loyal to a "state" (or more accurately, an identity), this "generational" conceptualization simply expands the definitional area that the term "militia" covers. Francis argues that these second-generation militias are still theoretically connected to previous understandings of the term because they consider themselves a force for good, but in the context of weak or failing states, these groups are often coopted by special interests.[10] This suggests that the terminology may offer little analytical difference between such "second-generation militias" and "rebels" or "insurgents." This arguably makes the use of the term "militia" less valuable. This work attempts a much broader sweep in understanding the DDR experience. While its focus is on less formally organized groups, there will be the occasional mention of cases of the DDR process on national military structures (notably South Africa at the end of Apartheid and Nepal after the electoral victory of the Maoists).

This work will focus on the DDR process for armed groups regardless of their position vis-à-vis the state. In fact, that position (whether in support of or against) is one of the factors requiring consideration when implementing DDR, as will be shown later in the book. Whether the group being demobilized is a "rebel" group, a "militia" in the traditional understanding of the term, or a formal military organization will have some bearing on its demobilization process regardless of the behavior of the individual personnel.[11] The "type" of group influences the *political* context for its DDR experience, if not the emotional or moral context for DDR and its associated processes (including longer-term reconciliation and peacebuilding). This political differentiation can be problematic, as Dudouet note a bias for restoring/preserving state structures over internal security reforms in UN peacebuilding guidelines. The bias is understandable, as the international community generally privileges "stability" over "security," and is generally hesitant to infringe on another member's sovereignty. Demobilizing a rebel group or even a citizen militia is one thing, demobilizing another country's standing military is something (politically) quite different. While this difference is understandable, Dudouet accurately points out that this bias can undermine the perceived legitimacy of the process, as

> [Non-State Armed Groups] tend to view the generic terminology and concepts of DDR . . . with suspicion, perceiving them as biased and imbalanced and chiefly concerned with dismantling nonstatutory forces and removing their capacity to engage in armed rebellion, whereas statutory forces can get away with minor reforms.[12]

For the purposes of this work, the term "irregular armed groups" or "irregular forces" is the generic term to encompass all of the groups under consideration here. Although many of these groups have a formal organizational structure, it is generally less rigid than national military forces, and their tactics and procedures are usually much more flexible. On the other hand, irregular armed groups are usually at a disadvantage in comparison with national forces in the areas of overall resources and logistical support. While the term "irregular forces" is not without its problems, it is sufficiently broad to contain those groups whose acts of violence and public statements articulate a challenge to or dismissal of the state mechanism and/or authority as well as those groups that support (or are used by) the government in power. This work will not cover extensively criminal organizations or other violent groups, such as gangs. While there may not be a definable demarcation between irregular armed groups and gangs in terms of levels of violence, some distinctions may be drawn. Some gangs may perform the same function as irregular armed groups such as providing a social system in areas where the government has failed; gangs generally lack the larger political agenda that irregular forces articulate. Gang violence may challenge the state or comment on its weakness, but that is not the purpose of said violence.[13] Irregular forces, on the other hand, generally have an understanding of their actions as a political or physical challenge to the state. In many cases, it is this political message that is the primary purpose of the violence. The phenomenon of sub-state groups taking up arms as a method to address grievances and challenge the state is not necessarily new, but the increasing spread of small arms (and the increasing lethality of those weapons) have made these groups significantly more dangerous (both to individuals and to the stability of existing governments) than they were in the past. Furthermore, the development of an armed "self-defense" group, even with the encouragement of the state, stands as testimony to the state's inability to proclaim a monopoly (or at least, preponderance) of violence.

The Implicit Criticism of Political Violence

The irony is that even when the armed group does not directly challenge the government, the authority and legitimacy of the state can be undermined. This is especially true in cases where the group is providing other services beyond security (such as medical care or education, most notably) to the population rather than those services being provided by the government. The existence of a militia group to provide for the security of a population suggests that the government cannot adequately protect its citizens. A group that not only provides security, but other social services is an even sharper critique of the government. (Indeed, in the latter case, to call the organization simply an "armed group" is a disservice to the group itself. Physical security is only one of many services it provides.) Regardless of whether the militia purports to support the government or not, the need for its existence reflects a perceived weakness of the state. A prominent example is Hezbollah in Lebanon. Hezbollah has not only been able to provide social services such as schools and public works to much of the Lebanese population, but it has also been able to establish itself (in public perception, at the very least) as the entity that provides military protection for Lebanon from Israel.[14] The viability of Hezbollah's claim that it provides for Lebanon's security and not the Lebanese military is an implicit criticism of the legitimacy of the Lebanese government.

Situating DDR in the Context of Peacebuilding

While the IDDRS program attempts to integrate the various phases of DDR, it must also be situated within a larger framework of building a stable post-conflict peace. In that sense, the phases of DDR should not just be related to each other, but the DDR process must be connected to several other programs or mechanisms. At the very least, these other programs include Small Arms and Light Weapons (SALW) reduction, Peacekeeping or Peacebuilding Operations, Security Sector Reform (SSR), Conflict Resolution, and Restorative Justice (RJ) arrangements. With the exception of Peacekeeping

Operations, the prevalent understanding by scholars is that most of these other processes take place *after* DDR. Boshoff states this explicitly in the case of the Democratic Republic of Congo, saying, "if the DDR process is not completed, the SSR process cannot start."[15] However, conceiving processes like SSR as taking place only after DDR is "completed" biases the short-term aspects of DDR, most notably, the disarmament phase. It is nonsensical to consider Security Sector Reform as beginning only after the "reintegration" of ex-combatants into society. Disarmament and the rest of the DDR process is a confidence-building measure that both enhances and is enhanced by the coordination and relationship with other programs building long-term peace after conflict. (Recent scholarship has stressed the need to connect and coordinate DDR and SSR,[16] but how to implement this is still up for debate.)

When considered against these other post-conflict programs, much of the prevailing scholarship focuses on DDR as a "short-term" enterprise. However, the very fact that "reintegration" is a long-term process highlights one of the major dilemmas in conceptualizing and understanding DDR. This combination of both short- and long-term goals is one of greatest challenges in conceptualizing DDR. (In some literature, the term "reinsertion" is being used and may be more accurate than defining "reintegration" as a process of six months to a year[17] or even upwards to five years.) Willibald accurately characterizes the dilemma, noting,

> on the one hand, disarmament and demobilization can be seen as constituting largely military affairs with the short-term objective of establishing security on the ground, thus creating space for other activities. On the other hand, reinsertion and reintegration can be seen as forming part of wider development affairs, with the long-term goal of reintegrating ex-combatants into communities.[18]

A more in-depth discussion of considering the "R" in DDR as a more long-term or short-term process is found in the reintegration chapter.

Many of the problems confronting implementation of truly effective DDR programs is recognizing those expediencies that have short-term benefit, but actually make the long-term goal of reintegration/post-conflict peace more difficult to achieve. A deeper consideration of whether to take the expedient route or to consider the longer-term implications is one of the most difficult problems in the DDR enterprise. The pressures of time are obviously at the heart of this problem. Resources are always finite, and priorities have to be developed, but it is not clear that lack of resources is the major problem in the success of DDR arrangements. A better understanding is that resources are far more abundant in the early stages and far less than needed later in the process. Simply put, resources are frequently more available during the disarmament process than later on in the reintegration phase.[19] Even in cases where the absolute level of funding is greater for reintegration, the planning and implementation for reintegration often is haphazard in UN programs because it is funded through voluntary contributions (while assessed contributions are used for the disarmament and demobilization phases),[20] and the international community may have lost interest in the problem as time goes on. Agencies (and associated governments) like shorter programs that are easier to build momentum for and are financially cheaper. Unfortunately, societal reintegration rarely runs on an electoral cycle. Furthermore, there clearly is oftentimes a lack of coordination between (and sometimes, within) governments and agencies. The competing agendas and mandates often diffuse the well-intentioned efforts of the various participants.

Besides such notions of time, the issue of the primary target in the DDR process should be considered. While much of the focus emphasizes the political aspects and agreements between states or states and sub-state actors, less attention has been paid to the ramifications of these agreements for the people at the grassroots level, and how the implementation of national agreements can stress the security environment at lower levels. Fundamentally, peacebuilding must be tied to security not just of the state, but also of its citizens, and DDR approaches must therefore understand the impact of their programs at the local and individual level. This concept of centering notions of security at the individual level has played a prominent part in the intellectual evolution of the DDR process. However, the implementation of the "human security" paradigm still proves elusive for government agencies.

Comprehensive and Human Security

The end of the Cold War allowed for the reconsideration of security issues, breaking free from much of the geopolitical calculations of the bipolar world system. Efforts were made to expand the idea of security and the consideration of threats to go beyond the narrow confines of a danger to the states' interests that may warrant a military response. With the bipolar conflict a thing of the past, new priorities could be considered for the international system, most notably in the expansion of development. Rather than focus simply on national production, however, an attempt was made to stress the idea of personal development. As part of this line of thought, the United Nations Development Programme (UNDP) issued its first Human Development Report in 1990.

Even beyond human development, issues such as transnational crime (to include money laundering and smuggling) had in some countries already become a major concern for their governments. Also, the spillover effects from these issues into other countries raised concerns for the stability of some regions. Even more widely, events or issues that did not have an "active" adversary (an opposing state, criminal gang, or terrorist organization) such as infectious disease or natural disasters were being considered as threats to a country's security. The term "comprehensive security" became widely used to differentiate these considerations from the traditional view of security, frequently called "national security." As a kind of subset to comprehensive security, the term "human security" also arose (the term is used in the UNDP's 1994 Report). More directly than the comprehensive security concept, human security directly noted that the individual, not the state, was the central referent to be considered when assessing security and the evaluation of threats. Human security therefore goes further than the traditional concept of "human rights" and suggests a significantly different understanding of security and the state's obligation to protect its populace. Human security also considers the involvement of a greater number and type of actors than traditional national security considerations. While traditional national security concerns have emphasized the central role of the state, human security recognizes the role of other agents (social movements, nonstate actors, international and intergovernmental organizations) in alleviating or exacerbating human security.

While an interesting theoretical perspective, the comprehensive/human security idea has remained problematic in terms of its implementation. First, if practically anything can be considered a "threat," then is anything a threat? Even if some things are "raised" to the level of "security threats," what is the proper response by a state to these expanded "threats"? Raising issues such as "food security" or infectious disease to the level of security issues may mean that they gain increased focus from political leaders (and with that, associated resources), but should that diminish the more traditional concerns of national defense? Despite these issues, efforts to consider security at the individual level are not only beneficial contributions to theory, but a pointed reminder to policymakers.

For Further Reading, See: United Nations Development Programme, Human Development Report, Oxford: Oxford University Press, 1994. All Human Development Reports are available online at http://hdr.undp.org.

The foremost concern in the immediate post-conflict situation is the prevention of a return to violence. Barring that, efforts that minimize the lethality and spectacle of that violence must be made. This is the consideration that drives the understandable emphasis on disarmament by DDR practitioners, especially in the early stages of the post-conflict environment. While understandable in theory, the differing contexts that DDR occurs in suggest a more considered understanding of the value (and meaning) of disarmament is in order.

CHAPTER THREE

Disarmament: The Ephemeral Beginning

The First Step?

The process of DDR, especially disarmament and demobilization, has a long history as a practice of war termination. With the conclusion of a decisive conflict, the disarmament process is relatively straightforward, at least in theory. The defeated party's armed forces are reduced in personnel and surplus weapons are taken away, usually destroyed. While easily expressed, the process is never perfect. Pockets of resistance may still exist, and the fear of retribution may cause some combatants on the defeated side to hide their weapons for their own personal protection. Programmatic DDR in the absence of a decisive victory, on the other hand, has been much more a phenomenon of the post Cold War era.[1] The removal of arms after an intrastate conflict where the opposing force is made up of militias or non-state armed groups also adds a level of complexity to the problem. Unlike an interstate war, the opposition force is not a "recognized" military and may not in fact have the formalized command structures expected of a regular military force. Having commanders "order" the disarmament of the forces under their command is difficult enough in formal forces; trying to do so in less recognized or solidified hierarchies can be even less successful. Finally, when there has not been a "decisive" end to the conflict, members of the opposing forces can be even less inclined to disarm, perhaps calculating that an outright victory is a possibility.

The need and attraction of the disarmament facet of DDR is obvious. Simply put, weapons are dangerous. While the Taliban's reasons for disarming opposing groups was in no way altruistic, Sedra notes that "it must be remembered that Taliban efforts to disarm militia groups and assert a monopoly over the use of force was their most popular policy."[2] However, a "post-conflict" situation does not automatically mean there will be peace. In fact, many cases have experienced an increase in "disorganized" violence as some combatants turn to criminality to make a living. Tensions still run high in the immediate aftermath of conflict, and the high concentration of weapons can easily make a bad situation worse. If a society has been experiencing a long period of violence, then violence becomes an "acceptable" response to resolving conflicts. It is also the case that prior cultural practices and traditions can become problematic when modern weaponry is added to the mix. Many cultures have long-standing practices of retribution[3] to settle disputes and restore "balance" in terms of righting wrongs. These codes of conduct, while certainly not applied uniformly or monolithically by any culture, have certainly been used often enough to be part of the understood patterns of behavior in the society. More importantly, these practices contributed to the maintaining of balance within the community, as illustrated by the insights of a coalition commander who worked in Afghanistan:

> Most societies engage only reluctantly in blood feuding – it's simply too costly. Not surprisingly, then, the whole system of Pashtunwali and Pashtun social interaction can sometimes be seen as a series of ways to prevent needing to execute "badal." In fact, it is often a series of systematic escalation, with an almost-endless string of negotiation and a long sequence of "off ramps" – a form of institutionalized brinksmanship [sic].[4]

These practices are designed to formalize the use of violence, but more critically, to *contain* it within manageable levels.

However, the increasing availability and lethality of small arms and light weapons has changed both the scale and impact of these past practices. Minor slights and misunderstandings combined with access to high-powered weapons can now more quickly lead to high casualties. The amount of violence that can be inflicted in a short time has compressed these social practices, making the time spent in negotiation (and the easing of tensions) shorter than in the past while the escalation of violence can occur more rapidly.[5] While removing weapons from the situation does not eliminate the violence, it does lower the potential for this quick escalation.

Beyond the physical need to remove weapons from an area of conflict, there is also a political attraction to disarmament. Disarmament is the most visible aspect of the entire DDR enterprise, and, simply put, disarmament certainly does look like "something" is happening. This political attraction of visible activity is certainly understandable, but it can bias governments and other institutions towards emphasizing the disarmament aspect of DDR over the deeper and more meaningful processes of demobilization and reintegration. The potential consequences of this bias will be covered later in this chapter.

The Process of Disarmament

Disarmament is officially defined as "the collection, documentation, control, and disposal of small arms, ammunition, explosives, and light and heavy weapons of combatants and often also of the civilian population. Disarmament also includes the development of responsible arms management programmes."[6] The IDDRS identifies four aspects to disarmament: (1) Information Collection and Operational Planning; (2) Weapons Collection; (3) Stockpile Management; and (4) Destruction.[7] Disarmament is ineffective without proper information collection. This information focuses on the physical and psychological aspects of disarmament. What estimates can be made about the number of weapons in the population? What type of weapons are prevalent in the area? Other physical factors include simple geography. What borders does the state have (land or maritime, mountainous or easily traversable) and how porous are they? Some geography makes cross-border flows easier or harder than others, but even the most difficult physical barriers will be overcome if there is enough need or desire. Without an adequate understanding of not only the internal society but also the regional factors involved, the most well-planned disarmament project will fail.

Recognizing the regional impact of disarmament programs includes two major factors. First, discussions frequently focus too much on the prevention of arms coming into the country. While this is certainly important to prevent the reinvigoration of the arsenals of the combatants, it does little to ease the situation moving into the post-conflict stage, since many weapons are already present in the area. Alpers points out that in the Pacific, the most common source of weapons are local police and defense force armories.[8] The second issue is the disarmament program having the unfortunate consequence of creating or exacerbating the regional arms trade. Edloe notes simply "well-executed national disarmament efforts have proven futile when no attention is paid to cross-border arms flows."[9] Arms flows can go both into and out of a country undergoing a disarmament program, and, given porous borders, combatants may simply search for the most financially beneficial program. Özerdem points out that a combatant surrendering a weapon in Liberia received $300 but weapons surrendered in neighboring Cote d'Ivoire garnered $900.[10] Indeed, considering the many porous border regions in the world, it is easy to be cynical about disarmament's effectiveness, but Berdal argues that even if borders cannot be sealed effectively, the symbolism of a sincere regional commitment can have an impact.[11]

Beyond these physical factors, there are psychological considerations for successful disarmament. What "value" does the weapon have in the cultural context of the combatants and the larger population? Is the possession of a weapon connected to rites of manhood or symbols of cultural strength? Are the weapons used for something other than killing other human beings (i.e., hunting)? Many analyses of specific cases have raised the argument that DDR has proven difficult to achieve due to a "culture" of violence that now permeates the situation. This argument over the consequences of a "gun culture" is addressed later in this chapter.

As part of information collection, the proper identification of combatants is critical for the appropriate implementation of disarmament. What individuals are considered "combatants" for the purposes of disarmament (and the associated incentives for demobilization and reintegration) is not always straightforward, but the effort to set clear and achievable criteria here is very important. If the criteria are too strict, many individuals will lose out (women forced into "marriage" with combatants, others who were not active fighters but provided other logistical support, etc.), but a too-expansive designation will increase the costs significantly.[12] The UNDPKO guidelines highlight some of these tensions, saying, "Any entrant who is unable to surrender any weapon or ammunition and is unable to prove combatant status should not be accepted for demobilization and reintegration" and immediately after noting, "Disarmament procedures that require weapons to be surrendered as a criterion for eligibility have often excluded children, especially girls."[13] Sedra says succinctly regarding Afghanistan, "the very definition of 'combatant' is problematic in the Afghan context."[14] He further points out that the working assumption by the UN for disarmament and demobilization in Afghanistan was about 75,000 individuals under clear command-and-control arrangements with perhaps another 100,000 irregular combatants. However, Deputy Defense Minister General Bismellah Khan gives a number of 500,000 individuals, with perhaps another 800,000 who wish to be integrated into the new Afghan armed forces.[15]

Another issue for identifying combatants has been the unfortunate growth in the level of conflict and associated weaponry. More than weapons handled by individuals, there is an increasing number of weapons "systems" that require more than one person to use. While the guidelines do consider various weapons and weapons systems, many programs are based on at least the implicit assumption of "one person-one weapon." This assumption can make the disarmament of teams that work heavier weapons such as mortars difficult if not all team members are viewed as having a weapon to turn in. Thruelson notes that in Afghanistan, for example, those fighters who were part of tank companies had some problems since they had no small weapons to surrender.[16] He further identifies in passing a similar problem seen in Liberia.[17] The effective identification of combatants has consequences for future demobilization and reintegration covered in later chapters, but the critical first assumption is that the identification of combatants as combatants is an important experience that allows both the individual and the community to move forward. This assumption is challenged by the experiences of female combatants in Sierra Leone. Ebbinghaus argues that many women and girl combatants refused to enter into disarmament and demobilization arrangements, because rather than allowing them to reintegrate back into civilian life, their declaration as a combatant would in fact cripple their ability to reenter traditional society.[18]

Weapons Collection

An often overlooked consideration during the weapons collection phase is the issue of ammunition in the conflict area. Unlike the weapons themselves, ammunition is not a reusable resource[19] and the amount (and type) of ammunition being collected provides significant insight into the progress of the disarmament program. Because many groups steal weapons (or sometimes buy them from corrupt members) of the security force, there is the obvious requirement to obtain the same type of ammunition. The bias towards American and NATO weapons in places like Bougainville, for example, are related to the fact that the Papua New Guinea Defence Force uses those weapons. Reports suggest that in the Pacific the presence of Kalashnikovs and the Chinese counterpart AK-47s has been muted, despite their durability and relative ease of use, due to the lack of available ammunition.[20] Mindanao in the Southern Philippines saw the same situation, resulting in fighters from the Moro National Liberation Front abandoning AK-47s.[21] A ready supply of ammunition can even create a market for homemade weapons. The high amount of .50-caliber ammunition left behind after World War II in much of the Pacific led to this latter practice, though at a smaller scale due to the relative ease with which a more modern weapon (and ammunition) could be obtained.[22] The stability of the .50-caliber munitions is an exception; the majority of the WWII .30-caliber rounds were "in poor condition and . . . 'unlikely to fire'."[23] Pézard also notes that lacking a consistent and reliable supply of ammunition can lead to commanders instilling (or at least, attempting to instill) greater "shooting discipline" on their subordinates.[24]

A greater focus on ammunition will enhance the disarmament phase. The identification of ammunition stockpiles can be easier than focusing on the weapons themselves. Using dogs trained to sniff out gunpowder are more likely to track ammunition, while new or well-cleaned weapons may escape their notice.[25] In the post-conflict phase, controlling the ammunition supply is an effective way to reduce the possibility of renewed conflict. British General Rupert Smith notes of his experience advising in Rhodesia/Zimbabwe:

> I had urged the ex-Rhodesians to equip the new battalions with their rifles, which fired NATO standard ammunition that only they had, rather than leaving them with the AK-47s that they had acquired in the bush, and for which there was no shortage of ammunition. The Rhodesians could not conceive of letting "these Terrs" [short for "terrorists"] have our weapons. As a result, when seven of these new battalions mutinied and started to kill each other on a tribal basis, we had the greatest difficulty in shutting down the violence, fuelled as it was by a ready supply of ammunition.[26]

Lowering the supply of ammunition also diminishes the lethality of the weapons still in the community. This opens the possibility of weapons remaining in the community for their symbolic value alone. Tensions involved in removing pieces of both symbolic and utilitarian value (weapons) may be lessened if simply ammunition is removed.

For the weapons themselves, there are two major components to collection. The first is collection "by command" and aimed at identified combatants and generally implemented by security forces (whether internal or peacekeeping forces). This type of disarmament is generally done under the auspices of some kind of peace agreement. The second component is collection "by consent" and refers to voluntary turn-in programs focused on the rest of the population rather than the combatants. These are sometimes referred to as "phase one" and "phase two" disarmament, but while they are frequently implemented in that order, this is not always the case. In rare situations, disarmament by consent occurs without a forcible removal of weapons. Furthermore, while disarmament by command is certainly important, it is success in disarmament by consent that indicates progress in the rest of the DDR process.

Disarmament by Command

Disarmament by command targets the combatants directly. The focus is on the assurance of basic security (the decrease, if not removal, of violent groups). The combatant is seen as a threat to the community that must be addressed before any other progress (most notably drawing the combatant back into society) is made. Removing weapons from those who will not surrender them willingly must have positive security benefits. Otherwise, this removal only increases resentment in the community, creating a larger potential number of intransigents. If the state is established as the legitimate provider of security for the entire populace, the transition for many combatants back into civilian life is eased.[27] However, this requires an understanding of the impacts of disarmament at the microlevel, the realm most frequently ignored in political negotiations. Most disarmament by command arrangements occur within the context of a peace agreement, macrolevel compromises can have significant microlevel impacts. Knight and Özerdem note that disarmament imperatives usually remain at the strategic and political level, with little consideration of the perception and needs of individual combatants.[28] Such agreements can even serve to exacerbate the conflict, as combatants can feel "doubly betrayed" by the government and their own rebel leadership. In that respect, "middle ranking" combatant leaders may bear special consideration, as they can prove the most effective "spoilers" in the developing peace process. In El Salvador, the top leadership of the *Frente Farabundo Marti para la Liberacion Nacional* (FMLN) needed more time to persuade this middle segment of the organization to support the peace process.[29] Rubin also highlights this problem in Afghanistan. While pointing out that this segment of the combatant population is very diverse and that general recommendations are difficult to formulate, Rubin does make some observations. He notes that these mid-level commanders will probably be the most difficult to demobilize due to internal and external factors. Many sub-commanders have grown wealthy due to drugs and other criminal activity and may prove reluctant to give up their power and prestige. Regarding external factors, Rubin argues "most are not promising material for the officer corps and are unlikely to make a career as politicians, since the local people hate them."[30] In that sort of situation, there is little reason for these mid-level commanders to view the cessation of conflict as personally beneficial.

Perhaps the single most critical insight regarding the disarmament phase of any DDR program is that the removal of weapons from a post-conflict society is not the end in and of itself. Given enough resources and backed by strong political will, coercive disarmament by a superior power over a lesser (or defeated) foe can be accomplished to a great, although never total, extent. A preoccupation with coercive disarmament, however, can lead to the resurgence of conflict or armed violence. This happens as combatants fight to hang on to the one clear resource they know they possess – their weapons. In addition, a disarmament program viewed as "too" coercive by the population can exacerbate resistance by creating a greater perception of insecurity and oppression. Removing weapons from the hands of the intransigent elements is important, but doing so in a way that will not push more people into insecurity and resistance is critical. The effects of "successful" disarmament can have detrimental impacts on future demobilization and reintegration programs, and this interplay will be covered in later chapters.

Disarmament by Consent

After the removal of weapons from intransigent elements, the next step is to continue to reduce the presence of weapons in the area by encouraging their voluntary handover. Practically all voluntary programs include some kind of incentive to encourage the handover of weapons. This can be unobtrusive, such as a general amnesty (no punishment for the illegal possession of weapons), but more usually include some type of payment for the weapon. Gun "buy-back" programs do not occur exclusively in post-conflict areas, but also take place in areas that experience high use of firearms in criminal activity or domestic disputes. In more unusual but memorable cases, a spectacular major event involving firearms have served as catalysts for a public debate on gun control. These events include the 1996 shootings of 16 primary school students and their teacher in Dunblane, Scotland by Thomas Hamilton, Martin Bryant's killing of 35 people in Port Arthur, Tasmania, the 1999 school shootings by Dylan Klebold and Eric Harris in Littelton, Colorado, and the 2007 shooting at Virginia Tech University by Seung-Hui Cho. In both Britain and Australia, gun control advocates pushed major campaigns for increased gun control and buy back programs in the aftermath of those events.

National Disarmament by Consent: The Case of Australia

Australia is a developed nation that has a viable and legitimate government and security forces. It is not a developing nation that is emerging from a long period of armed violence. However, Australia's domestic disarmament program provides some interesting insights in how to accomplish the goal of a national weapon turn-in within a liberal-democratic state. On April 28, 1996, Martin Bryant

---

went on a shooting spree in Port Arthur, Tasmania, killing 35 people. Bryant used two semi-automatic rifles for
his shootings, and investigations revealed that the pur-
chases were made with no licenses. The horror of the event
sparked a national debate over a gun control program.
The concern after Port Arthur shootings included how to
lower the number of guns already out in the population. In
response, the Howard Government eventually developed a
national buyback program. The weapons were surrendered
and the owners were paid a specified amount. Most of the
weapons were destroyed, with a few rare models being
donated to museums. Additionally, the program included
tighter requirements on weapons ownership, so while
some gun owners who surrendered weapons did purchase
others; it became more difficult to do so.

The Port Arthur tragedy notwithstanding, many opponents, especially anti-gun control groups, were highly
critical of the national program. The government was
accused of taking advantage of the community's emotional
response to forward an agenda. The tensions increased
when Prime Minister Howard, speaking to a group of
gun owners, could clearly be seen wearing a bulletproof
vest under his suit jacket. That image proved troubling, as
indignant gun owners from all over Australia considered
that a direct insult. However, despite that setback, Prime
Minister Howard was a politician of long experience and,
more importantly, had great credibility among the more
conservative elements of Australian society. While the
tragedy did allow the government to shape the debate and
stigmatize guns, especially high-velocity automatic weapons, to a level that was not achievable previously, the fact
that the gun control program was being pushed under the
more socially conservative of the major parties in Australia
enhanced its political and societal viability.

> Further Reading: Simon Chapman, *Over Our Dead Bodies: Port Arthur and Australia's Fight for Gun Control* (London: Pluto Press, 1998).

Debates in the United States have not led to the same level of stringent nationwide legislation, due mostly to Constitutional restrictions. Faltas, McDonald and Waszink argue that the success of weapons collection program in the United Kingdom and Australia related not only to the ability of groups to stigmatize guns after a major tragedy but also the tight weapons control associated with the new legislation.[31]

While these buyback programs have enjoyed great visibility and notoriety, scholarship is divided on whether the programs have a significant impact on the reduction of gun violence or suicide.[32] The first problem is the permanence of any program. The ability to replenish the supply of weapons in an area can render any gun surrender program meaningless. Secondly, the use of monetary incentives to purchase weapons may motivate "former" combatants to turn in their weapons, but does not prevent them from purchasing new ones. Willibald argues that cash incentives do have value in the DDR project, but that "cash fails to meet adequately the contextual challenges that arise during the disarmament stage of DDR."[33] Willibald accurately identifies a significant problem to cash incentives for disarmament – these incentives can cause community resentment in that they seemingly "reward" combatants with cash for weapons. This image is troubling for a variety of reasons. Politically (and in some cases, morally), it is problematic for any peace process to reward combatants. Even the perception of doing so can cripple progress in reconciliation and reintegration. More pragmatically, a cash-for-weapons scheme can encourage regional arms flows and corruption. Willibald notes:

This finding is echoed in other studies, suggesting that cash payments should perhaps be spatially and temporarily [sic] disconnected from disarmament and demobilisation. However, seeing that former combatants should not return to communities empty-handed and given the need to provide some sort of "inducement" to disarm, an effective solution to reconcile beneficiaries' needs with the imperative to avoid a cash-for-weapons image is yet to be found when deciding on payment location.[34]

This recognition that cash payments are detrimental in the disarmament phase of DDR can be more accurately described as the problem of cash incentives in the *early* stages of DDR, regardless of what "phase" is being implemented. In the early and still-uncertain phase of the DDR project, combatants frequently are still focused on short-term benefits. The use of cash benefits in this early stage only exacerbates the tension in the area, creating a "market" for weapons that does little to decrease the societal tensions present. Because cash is an easily exchangeable commodity, it can be used to repurchase other (likely more effective) weapons, thus proving of little benefit to the security situation. Cash incentives are of greater benefit later in the DDR process, after relationships of trust have been built and are growing. The issue is not the effectiveness of cash incentives, but timing their implementation. The real factor that determines their value (and indeed, determines the value of the disarmament phase writ large) is the nurturing of relationships of trust among all of the parties.

A Matter of Trust

The ability to offer incentives to get people to turn in weapons is important, but while these incentives matter, the "real" reason disarmament works is trust. Spear points out that credible, effective policing is critical for disarmament programs to work. The State (or some other credible actor) has to provide security for the population so the militias and/or public do not see themselves as justified in doing so.[35] Knight and Özerdem argue, "By disarming, the combatants are forging a new social contract with the government and international community – the combatants surrender the security and economic surety that their weapons provide, in exchange for opportunities and assistance in finding new peaceful livelihoods."[36] Spear's "effective policing" is more than the capability of the force to ensure security, however, it also means the trust needed that the police will not prove to be a destabilizing force. Faltas, McDonald and Waszink refer to this as the "dual effort to improve the capacity of the state to enforce the law, on the one hand, and to create effective safeguards against the abuse of state power, on the other."[37]

Trust is the significant theme running through disarmament programs (indeed, for DDR programs overall) and their contribution to a lasting peace. Trust in the process means either a tentative confidence that the opposing side(s) will not renege or that a neutral third party exists to maintain or provide security, as well as act as a buffer between opposing groups. Certainly, the May 1993 discovery of an FMLN arms cache in neighboring Nicaragua (the discovery was made when the arsenal accidentally exploded) proved embarrassing for the FMLN and the United Nations. The UN Secretary-General had already declared the FMLN completely disarmed. The FMLN subsequently turned over more than a hundred caches from El Salvador, Nicaragua and Honduras, by August 1993, accounting for about 30 percent of the FMLN's arsenal.[38] These caches continued to be found up until 2001.[39] All parties acted impressively despite this setback, and the fact that disarmament was not the first step in the reintegration of the FMLN, but came about after an atmosphere of trust had already developed no doubt contributed positively (see Text Box later in this chapter). The reintegration of the FMLN into Salvadoran society continued, culminating in the election of FMLN party leader Mauricio Funes as President in 2009. (Funes himself was not a former combatant, but his rise to the party leadership is also indicative of the evolving of the FMLN from its Marxist and violent past and the reintegration of its members into the larger society.)

Trust is obviously difficult to foster between two parties that have been in conflict over a long period. In the case of third-party interventions, the issue of perceived neutrality may be the most valuable social capital any intervention force has in dealing with the opposing parties. The effort to suppress the violence by both the Rhodesian Security Forces and their opponents the Rhodesian Patriotic Front was taken under the auspices of the Commonwealth and was, for the most part, a unilateral action on the part of the British, who had relationships with parties on both sides of the conflict. These relationships were problematic at times for the British, as neither side viewed the British forces as impartial. The Patriotic Front thought that the Brits had "secret deals" with the Rhodesians, while the Rhodesians thought the Brits were betraying white "solidarity."[40] The British approach to "disarming" the conflicting groups in Rhodesia was not disarmament at all. Rather, they established a meaningful physical separation between the parties. This separation provided the political and emotional "breathing space" for trust to develop. This ability to forgo disarmament may not be available in most situations, but it bears consideration in areas with amenable geography.

Trading Space for Disarmament: The Case of Rhodesia/ Zimbabwe

An interesting approach to the disarmament problem was implemented in Rhodesia (soon to become Zimbabwe) during its break from minority white rule. The British (who practically ran this operation unilaterally) were reluctant to engage in a more traditional peacekeeping operation, as that would entail greater numbers of personnel and time than they were willing to commit. The British viewed their mission as facilitating and monitoring more than peace-keeping. The approach to the disarmament question here was to use physical space and distance to overcome the presence of weapons. Instead of putting a peacekeeping force between the belligerent parties (the exact thing the British did not want to do and did not have the personnel to do), the idea was to separate the parties geographically as much as possible. It would be this distance itself that would serve as the buffer between the competing parties. Many of the combatants were allowed to keep their weapons, but because there were no adversaries nearby, there was no need to use the weapon. The ability to establish geographic separation meant the weapons were less capable of spark-ing a potential conflict. This helped build the trust between the combatants, rather than an ill-suited disarmament program. Arguably, the lesson here is not strictly about dis-armament, but creating the conditions for demilitarization, and approaching the latter goal via the separation and dis-engagement of rival forces. This psychological separation from the militarized mindset is critical in the demobili-zation of forces, and the Rhodesia/Zimbabwe case study suggests opportunities to begin this demobilization with-out significant disarmament.

> Further reading: Jeremy Ginifer, *Managing Arms in Peace Processes: Rhodesia/Zimbabwe* (Geneva: United Nations Institute for Disarmament Research, 1995).

Establishing and maintaining trust is a psychological endeavor. What actions actually build trust is not universal between conflicts or involved parties. For example, attempting to treat all groups "equally" will almost certainly raise some tensions. The issue is one of perceived status and respect. More specifically, state-sanctioned security forces are highly reluctant to be equated with irregular groups. Irrespective of the relative level of organization or fighting effectiveness, uniformed service members nearly always view themselves as superior to irregular groups. In corollary to this, irregular groups either want to be viewed as equal or even superior to the official security forces. In the former case, the irregular group usually is fighting against the security force. The same can be true in the latter case, but the group may also claim superiority since it provides something the security force does not (protection of the population from other threats). In Rhodesia, the Rhodesian security forces objected to being treated essentially the same as those they considered "rebels" in the Patriotic Front. In East Timor, the Australians found themselves dealing with the objection of the Falintil [*Forças Armadas da Libertação Nacional de Timor-Leste*, The Armed Forces for the National Liberation of East Timor] to disarm as opposing Indonesian militias (though many were armed by the Indonesian government, they were not officially part of the military) would do the same. Falintil commanders are promised that the pro-Indonesian militias will disarm 48 hours after the Falintil are disarmed and its members placed in cantonment sites, but the commanders still resist. The emotional component of disarmament was significant; it amounted to handing weapons over to the enemy. The Indonesian government viewed the Falintil as a rebel/separatist force, and the pro-Indonesian militias as self-defense groups. However, rather than viewing themselves as a "rebel force," the Falintil considered themselves the beginnings of the soon-to-be independent East Timor security force. Cristalis notes:

> Disarmament in East Timor never escaped this impasse. The [pro-Indonesia] militias were still flaunting their weapons openly. The Indonesians kept insisting that the existence of these groups was a direct reaction to the activities of Falintil and that they would disarm if Falintil did so as well. But Falintil refused to see itself equated in this way with the militias. They were East Timor's armed forces, and if there had to be an equivalent it was the Indonesian army.[41]

Being recognized as a "militia" carries a certain amount of political prestige, more than being a "rebel," and certainly more than a "terrorist."[42] Many group leaders recognize this perception and will resist giving up that standing. Conversely, negotiators must consider this labeling and the level of legitimacy it gives the group in relation to the various audiences (domestic, regional, and international) that are watching.

Stockpile Management and/or Destruction

The next step deals with the management of the collected weapons. Regardless of what will ultimately be done with them, the collection phase creates a situation where a large number of weapons will be in a relatively small area. This can provide a tempting target for any potential spoilers to the peace process. Any collected weapons that "leak" back out into the populace lowers the credibility of the collection program and the entire DDR mission (and its agents) more generally. Often, governments plan to use the surrendered weapons in the reconstituted security force. In such a case, a plan for weapons storage is required, and security and trust are major issues. The 1992 UN Mission in Mozambique's weapon collection program did not destroy the weapons but planned to transfer them to the new Mozambique Defense Force. However, the storage was not well secured and many weapons found their way back on the streets.[43] So called "double key" systems require two keys to open the collected armory, with one key held by an irregular force commander and the other by a government official or international monitor, and are a popular way to insure the stockpile's security and build confidence between the parties. The effectiveness of this system relies on the security of the keys (limited possession, inability to be copied, etc.) and in some cases, the literal structure where the stored weapons are kept. Mozambique implemented this double key system, but Berman called the locks mostly a "symbolic" deterrent.[44] Dzinesa points out that in Angola, stockpiles were kept in tents and grass huts, making any kind of lock and key system useless.[45] Mozambique also had a secondary problem regarding its stockpiles. The weapons collected were to be classified as "operational, repairable, or beyond repair," but since it had been decided that weapons destruction would not be economically feasible, all of the weapons were simply turned in regardless of condition.[46]

Beyond the physical security of the stockpile storage area, the trust between the respective parties is much more important in securing the weapons. In situations where such trust is precarious, the value of weapons preservation is generally outweighed by the cost of storage and protection. Security and trust are increased with the destruction of the collected weapons. Weapons destruction addresses the physical reality of the level of weaponry in the area but perhaps more importantly has a psychological impact. This impact is most significant with the use of public destruction programs. Destroying surrendered weapons delivers the obvious but powerful message that these specific weapons will no longer be part of the cycle of violence. Doing so publicly assures the community that the weapons have in fact been destroyed. Furthermore, public destruction of weapons can be connected to ceremonies or celebrations for peace and be an initial part of the reconciliation and reintegration process. In Mali, some three thousand weapons were burned in the "Flame for Peace."[47] Local participation in public destruction programs and ceremonies was particularly encouraged during the intervention in the Solomon Islands.

Public Weapons Destruction: The Regional Assistance Mission to the Solomon Islands (RAMSI)

The Solomon Islands is an island group northeast of Australia. Since the mid-1990s tensions have grown on the main island of Guadalcanal between the indigenous Gwale (also known as the Isatabu) and people from neighboring island of Malaita. Malaitans had migrated to Guadalcanal for economic opportunities, but could not own land there. Malaitans dominated the political and economic infrastructure on Guadalcanal, and resentment grew from the Gwale, who formed a militia (the Isatabu Freedom Movement). In response, the Malaitans formed the Malaitan Eagle Force, and obtained a great deal of weapons from the predominantly Malaitan Solomons Islands Police Force. Incidents of violence increased, culminating in the forceful removal of Prime Minister Ulufa'alu in June 2000. In 2003, Australia led a multinational task force to quell this violence. RAMSI is an excellent illustration of the value of public ceremonies and displays of weapons destruction. It is also an example of institutional learning and adaptation.

Australian armed forces had acquired a great amount of experience in peacekeeping operations in the Oceania region through the 1990s, and two lessons in particular are of great importance. In the first, Australia followed New Zealand's lead in the Bougainville region in Papua New Guinea. New Zealand first led a Truce Monitoring Group (TMG) to separate the actors involved in the secessionist movement on Bougainville. The TMG would evolve into the Peace Monitoring Group with Australia in the lead. New Zealand's TMG was an unarmed mission. This fact put the security of the monitors in the hands of the conflicting parties and built trust among the parties. Australia's follow up was also an unarmed mission, though many in the Australian military were uncomfortable with this idea.

The second experience was Australia's work in East Timor. East Timor had voted for independence from Indonesia and Australia led the regional (later UN-authorized) mission to handle the transition to independence. Part of the agreement required the disarmament of the various militias in East Timor (although there was great debate as to what groups constituted "militias"). Understandably, many Timorese feared that any weapons they surrendered would wind up in the hands of the Indonesian militias and/or the military. As such, many pro-independence combatants proved extremely reluctant to surrender weapons to the peace operation.

Considering the Bougainville experience, it was tempting to structure a mission along those lines again. However, the discomfort of many soldiers contributed to the heavy initial RAMSI deployment. Rather than relying on the conflicting parties to protect the intervention force, RAMSI would provide its own security. Recognizing the different contexts of Bougainville and RAMSI also made a heavily armed intervention force a more appropriate approach. Using the conflicting parties to guarantee the safety of the TMG in Bougainville built confidence and trust among parties that had been fighting for over a decade. The situation in the Solomons was still quite new and uncertain, making the trust-building mechanism of an unarmed mission far more dangerous than in Bougainville.

Recognizing the lesson of East Timor, RAMSI opted to conduct mass weapons destruction ceremonies rather than contribute to an already distrustful situation. The ceremonies were held with great visibility. The destruction methods were relatively simple (using electric saws to cut rifles in half) and village leaders were frequently brought up to help with the destruction. Large celebrations would follow, as the destroyed weapons would be piled together, frequently in the center of the village.

Further Reading: Jon Fraenkel, *The Manipulation of Custom: From Uprising to Intervention in the Solomon Islands* (Wellington: Victoria University Press, 2004), and Russell W. Glenn, *Counterinsurgency in a Test Tube: Analyzing the Success of the Regional Assistance Mission to Solomon Islands (RAMSI)* (Santa Monica: RAND, 2007).

There are a few logistical considerations for weapons destruction. Some destruction methods are more complete than others. For example, plugging the firing chamber can "destroy" a weapon, but it is not impossible to replace the gun chamber or in some cases, to actually remove the plugging material. In other cases, the removal of the firing pin does not permanently disarm the weapon. These weapons may be better referred to as "disabled" rather than "destroyed." Such was the case in Sierra Leone in 2000, and the disabled weapons were quickly brought back into circulation after the breakdown of peace negotiations.[48] Also, while destroying weapons can be done relatively safely with crude devices (chainsaws, for example), destroying ammunition is significantly more dangerous and requires more technical expertise. Even if the ammunition is no longer viable to be fired, the gunpowder can still explode.

Overstating Disarmament's Promise?

Because disarmament looks like "something" is happening, it is arguably given greater weight than it deserves in the evolution of the peace process. There is little doubt that all other things being equal, the removal of weapons in a situation of high-tension and unresolved differences is a beneficial thing, but disarmament in and of itself is not necessarily a resolution. Focusing on the achievements of the disarmament phase can distort the sense of achievement and diminish funding for other projects that are more significant in the establishment of a long-term peace. Muggah says rightly, "Time and time again funding for 'reintegration' activities is curtailed from the beginning and resources directed instead to more 'visible' interventions, such as the collection of firearms."[49] Disarmament programs are frequently used as the greatest measure of success in evaluating a DDR program, but it truly only scratches the surface of the problem. Apparently, disarmament is so successful in many cases that it occurs over and over again. Muggah writes, "Donors and governments continue to prioritize, even fetishize, the gathering of hardware. This 'disarmament bias' persists despite growing evidence that absolute numbers of arms collected do no[t] necessarily contribute to improved security, or even the building of confidence."[50] Measuring the progress of a DDR program by focusing on disarmament is the equivalent of measuring progress in insurgencies by the number of casualties. This infamous "body count" measure is as dubious in measuring the effectiveness of disarmament programs as it is when evaluating a counterinsurgency.

Disarmament may be the "first step" in building a lasting peace, but it is only a step. Indeed, it may not even be the first step at all. The assumption that DDR proceeds in logical, phased progression manifested in visible accomplishments (such as the collection of weapons) misses the more psychological aspects of a successful program. Peace negotiations are themselves confidence building measures, and to jeopardize the process by insisting on the prominence of a single factor (i.e. disarmament) misses the point. Disarmament may be the foundation for trust, but trust may also be the foundation for disarmament.

Trust Before Disarmament: El Salvador

The general argument in negotiating peace agreements is the need for a clear disarmament program. This program, the argument goes, will build trust between the parties and enable further progress on other issues, such as demobilization and eventual reconciliation and reintegration. The theory that disarmament builds trust is understandable, but the reverse has also been true in practical application. This point is made starkly in the case of El Salvador. Rather than address the widespread presence of arms in the community, the government and the FMLN decided to negotiate on other matters first. The disarmament of the FMLN was in fact the *last* decision point in the peace agreement. Rather than disarmament being the foundation for increased trust and demobilization of the FMLN, the trust built from continual negotiations (and the perceived fairness of those negotiations) led to greater inclination from the FMLN to disarm.

While the El Salvador case shows the power of trust, the influence of outside factors must also be recognized. The FMLN becomes increasingly amenable to negotiations with the Salvadoran government towards the end of the Cold War. The loss of the material support from the Soviet Union (directly or via Cuba) cannot be discounted in the FMLN's calculations and desire for a negotiated settlement. Nevertheless, these outside factors help establish the context of the negotiations, but they do not determine their result, and there is little question that the very process of the negotiations themselves led to a situation where the FMLN membership felt secure enough to discuss the surrender of weapons.

Further reading: Cate Buchanan and Joaquín Chávez, "Guns and Violence in the El Salvador Peace Negotiations," Negotiating Disarmament Country Study 3 (Geneva: Centre for Humanitarian Dialogue, March 2008).

A great deal more than the physical removal of weapons has to occur for situations to progress towards peace, and the ability of organizations to coordinate their activities (and their goals) would certainly go a long way in enhancing this process. Scholars argue that one of the most significant bureaucratic obstacles in the greater integration of the DDR process is the World Bank's stance. The Bank's Operational Principles do not allow it to fund disarmament programs.[51] Others argue that the problem is in fact deeper. The problem is not with the lack of funding, but a conflict of vision between the World Bank and other organizations. Dzinesa points out that while the Bank does not fund disarmament, the real issue is that the Bank's programs for reconstruction tend to disadvantage the former combatant. He cites the examples of Sierra Leone and Liberia, where it proved more profitable for combatants to rearm rather than continue under the World Bank's demobilization programs.[52] Even the case for coordination and integration of agencies and the DDR process may not be the universal answer. The problem has another dimension – the ability to clearly separate "citizens" from "combatants." While conceding that in cases where the distinctions are clear, more integrated approaches may be more beneficial, Jennings offers the provocative idea that the delinking of disarmament and demobilization programs from reintegration may increase the effectiveness of both programs in more ambiguous situations. Her research and interviews with ex-combatants in Liberia suggest a general dissatisfaction among the ex-combatants that the promises made for reintegrating them into society were not kept. She suggests that the high level people falsely identifying as combatants to gain monetary reward for turning in weapons or otherwise qualifying for other benefits overloaded the system.[53] Jennings then argues that "delinking [disarmament and demobilization from reintegration] may be a way to 'satisfy' [combatants] by providing an immediate, concrete reinsertion benefit, without creating false or unfulfilled expectations."[54] However, the value of delinking the programs has to do with the difficulty in accurately identifying combatants in the Liberian case. Cases where the combatants can be accurately identified lessens the possibility of overloading the program's personnel and/or its resources with frauds attempting to receive benefits, but it will not lessen the strain if there are a large number of legitimate former combatants requiring assistance.

Delinking the DDR phases in ambiguous situations can also reinforce the idea that reintegration programs are not "rewards" for combatants (a point discussed in greater detail in the reintegration chapter) while also providing some necessary material assistance. Without the ability to delineate clearly combatants from the rest of the society, the Liberian case suggests that people will identify as combatants in an effort to obtain reintegration benefits. Jennings writes, "Because ex-combatants received benefits by virtue of being ex-combatants, claiming the label became attractive for many similarly impoverished. Thus, in a society with few functioning services, DDR created a market for ex-combatants."[55] Accurate and equitable identification of combatants is perhaps the greatest bureaucratic challenge in the disarmament and demobilization stages.

Culture of the Gun

Discussions of disarmament frequently point to the gun as a tangible resource, as a source of protection, a badge of authority, or simply a symbol of power. In the last instance, the gun has less to do with its actual physical reality than as a symbol of power and (more specifically in some cases) manhood. In some societies in Chad, Alusala notes, " it is considered an abomination for a young initiate not to own a gun, while the ability to defend oneself with the weapon is considered a sign of unparalleled prowess."[56] The possession of a firearm is too deeply tied to cultural mythologies of manhood, virility, and power to be surrendered easily.[57] If those ties are truly salient, then firearms possession will not be relinquished simply because the security situation improves, but individuals will continue to possess firearms for other reasons. Frequently, analysis of DDR projects in countries will point to this "gun culture" as a larger problem for progress in disarmament. Those societies that have incorporated the gun into their expressions of power and authority, or are said to glorify physical violence, have deeper, more intractable obstacles to disarmament than simply the physical value or utility of the weapon itself. For example, Sedra refers to Afghans' refusal to participate in disarmament programs as "inate."[58] If such is the case, then any disarmament program proves to be highly problematic, to say the least. (On the other hand, understanding the status of weapons *possession* may not automatically correspond to weapons *use*. Anecdotally, Briggs notes that during his time in Afghanistan, the fact that nearly every male carried a weapon simply became part of the background. Briggs refers to the guns as "accessories".)[59]

The idea of a "gun culture" is an interesting headline and a provocative theme in less formal pieces by noted scholars. For example, Eric Hobsbawm in a lecture referred to Colombia and Mexico as "naturally bloodthirsty" cultures.[60] Regarding more academic analysis, what is interesting about the explanation is that these cultures can apparently be found in areas all over the world.[61] While the "culture of the gun/culture of violence"[62] assertion is frequently made, it has not generally been backed by much actual data. A systematic attempt to examine the connection between a so-called "gun culture" and gun possession in Southeastern Europe suggests that the motivations for gun ownership have very little to do with amorphous concepts of "culture" and "tradition." The report states that these ideas are "not a principal reason for gun ownership . . . Except in Montenegro, where 21.8 percent of respondents believed that 'tradition' was the main reason people owned guns in their local area. In other countries or territories in the region, only one percent to five percent of respondents cited 'tradition' as the most common reason for gun possession, opting for reasons of personal or property protection instead."[63] Interestingly, Waldmann has argued that this very lack of data makes an even *stronger* case for a gun culture's existence. Using the Colombia case, he argues that the values are so deeply internalized that respondents did not consciously recognize them as motivations for gun possession.[64] The results of the polling data would be therefore be the same, but the interpretations very different. (This "evidence by absence" is an intriguing line of investigation, but requires an examination of corollary issues that could distinguish between these competing explanations that is beyond the scope of the current work.)

Most culturalist arguments have focused on the connection between weapons and notions of manhood, but have not sufficiently investigated the notion of masculinity itself. Kimberly Theidon has given greater consideration of the connection of what she calls "militarized masculinity – that fusion of certain practices and images of maleness with the use of weapons"[65] with weapons possession. She argues that DDR practices have been lacking in their consideration of gender, using the term simply as a replacement for "female." While certainly not dismissing the consideration of women for DDR, Theidon argues that a more conscious examination of the masculine would also improve the DDR program. Theidon calls for "changing the configuration of practices that signify not only what it means to be a man, but also what it means to be *good at being a man.*"[66] Theidon's argument is a more serious attempt to take cultural values into account when considering the viability of disarmament. A more conscious understanding of notions of masculinity and what aspects can be emphasized to reduce violence rather than glorify it would greatly enhance the effectiveness of any disarmament program. More deeply, Theidon's analysis should point those negotiating and implementing a DDR program to give consideration to the psychological shifts by the ex-combatants required for success. Simply put, the voluntary (partly motivated by rewards or otherwise) surrendering of weapons *means something.* It suggests a step away from dispute resolution and security through violence and hope for a more peaceful society. It suggests the demobilization of the irregular forces.

CHAPTER FOUR

Demobilization: The Real Heart of the Matter

The Real First Step

The disproportionate focus on disarmament is to the detriment of the deeper issues of the DDR project. The visibility of weapons removal/collection/destruction cause many to overemphasize its importance when, arguably, it may be the easiest aspect of the DDR enterprise. Indeed, many of the cases suggest that disarmament is not the first step in the peace process, but that other factors (such as space, fatigue, or tentative agreements on other, less critical issues) can encourage or even replace disarmament. The building of trust between parties may come about as a result of disarmament, but it is also possible (arguably, even likely) that trust leads to disarmament. While establishing a secure environment from which to implement further operations is an understandable point of focus, there is no automatic connection between disarmament and that secure environment.[1] Care must therefore be taken in understanding *what disarmament represents* and not overstate its value. As Maulden says, "while post-conflict disarmament or demilitarization removes weapons from non-army and possibly even army fighters, it does not subsequently take the willingness or desire to use them out of child or adult hearts and minds."[2] Is disarmament a process occurring in a situation of uncertainty and distrust, perhaps imposed upon the competing parties by outside forces, or is it a product of long negotiation, building upon evolving relationships of trust? Is disarmament, in fact, an expression of the *psychological demobilization* of the combatants?

The 1999 DPKO defined demobilization as simply "the process by which armed forces (government and/or opposition or factional forces) either downsize or completely disband, as part of a broader transformation from war to peace."[3] The IDDRS expands the definition further. In the IDDRS, demobilization is "the formal and controlled discharge of active combatants from armed forces or other armed groups. The first stage of demobilization may extend from the processing of individual combatants in temporary centres to the massing of troops in camps designated for this purpose (cantonment sites, encampments, assembly areas or barracks). The second stage of demobilization encompasses the support package provided to the demobilized, which is often called reinsertion."[4] Thus, the IDDRS attempts to merge the end of demobilization with the beginnings of the reintegration phase. Evaluating the progress of the demobilization of combatants may be a better indicator of the level of trust between the conflicting parties than the number of weapons surrendered. More than the removal of weapons, the removal of command systems (although not necessarily the relationships between former commanders and subordinates) and reduction of the psychological state of "combat" is more important in establishing the foundations for long-term peace. Understanding this places demobilization as the true core of the DDR project.

Shifting Focus to Demobilization: The Delicate Handover

A government's decision to mobilize an armed force is fraught with societal tensions. In general, a time of war raises the need for compromises between the upper and working classes, with the latter now more in demand for their "usual" services (since their supply will drop as some enter into the military). The working class then achieves certain social and political gains. The question in the post-war situation is whether those gains will be consolidated or reversed. Campbell writes succinctly, "States may conscript soldiers to fight foreign enemies, but in doing so they simultaneously arm a potential internal opposition."[5] Conflicts "internal" to a state magnify this tension, since the concept of "national loyalty" is contested in the first place. The ability of the national government to earn and keep the loyalty of the population is the objective. In a post-conflict situation, outside states and other agencies often try to support this by insuring national "ownership" of the DDR program. At the end of the day it will be the domestic government that has to deal with longer-term issues of reconciliation and reintegration. As such, the government must be seen by the population as being "in control" of the DDR program. However, this cannot be done artificially. In the case of Afghanistan, where the very idea of national identity is questionable, there is little value in pushing the national "ownership" of the program. In fact, for Afghanistan a high level of national direction can be counterproductive, as sub-state (and alternative) levels of governance can view the national government as acting illegitimately or unfairly.[6] In such cases, too much deference to the national level by international actors can hinder the process, as national actors may be biased or corrupt. However, without at least some acceptance at lower levels of the DDR program, subordinate officials or other authority figures can block implementation. Thruelsen therefore argues for national "buy-in" or "acceptance" rather than "ownership."[7]

Operationally, the shift in focus towards demobilization (assuming a period of disarmament has already occurred) implies (at least psychologically) a shift from military-led operations to increasing involvement (and perhaps leadership) from civilian agencies. In military parlance, demobilization carries an expectation that the military will move from being the "supported" agency to being one of the "supporting" agencies. Managing this handover requires great skill. Military and security forces cannot simply depart when overt violence ends, thinking their job is done. While the security situation has become less threatening, there is always the potential for spoilers to reignite the violence. Successful military/security force departures are part of a larger psychological shift removing the use of violence from the acceptable avenues of settling disputes.

Which "D" Comes First? This Is Not the Question

Even in the cases where a disarmament program is the first visible phase of a peace process, deeper investigation suggests that other, more internal/psychological shifts occurred first. These shifts were then either made manifest in disarmament or in some cases encouraged a second stage of further weapons removal. The power of a "gun culture" in many countries can make the potential for large-scale, "commanded" disarmament problematic, but even if credence is given to such cultural arguments, they are not necessarily obstacles for demobilization. "Gun cultures" place value on the possession of weapons for a variety of reasons, many of which (prestige and symbolic power, in particular) can have little to do with a gun as an actual (rather than potential) provider of security. Confidence that agents of the state can and will provide this security evenly and effectively either allows irregular forces to demobilize on their own, or grants the larger public greater latitude to shame them into doing so. Thus, while disarmament may still prove difficult due to cultural factors rather than perceptions of security, demobilization may not pose the same problem. Rather than demobilization being the stage that follows disarmament, understanding disarmament as the physical manifestation of an ongoing psychological demobilization process may offer greater insight into the overall DDR process at the microlevel. In Mozambique, for example, negotiations for disarmament were not seriously considered until demobilization was significantly underway.[8] The example of El Salvador in the previous chapter also shows how negotiations and the building of trust lead to disarmament, rather than extend from it. This also emphasizes the point that demobilization can begin even without total disarmament (since "total" disarmament is an impossibility, the point is that demobilization *always* occurs in an environment of incomplete disarmament).

Indeed, the earlier discussion of disarmament "by consent" easily fits into understanding that kind of disarmament as a representation of demobilization. In fact, a "followup" disarmament project enacted after the initial DDR programs could reinforce initial success. Maulden points to the 2005 "Arms for Development" program in Sierra Leone run by the United Nations Development Programme, which is initiated long after the conclusion of the formal DDR process. Recognizing that DDR programs are chronically underfunded (especially in the later stages), she suggests that "a late[r] microdisarmament program facilitates the roundup of more weapons while enlarging local capacities for social and economic rehabilitation and integration."[9] These programs can generally follow some time after the formal process and be led by more local organizations with a longer-term commitment to building a peaceful community in the area.

In the end, whether disarmament must follow demobilization or vice versa is not the significant question. Whatever the sequence, there should be a mutually reinforcing link between the two facets of the DDR project. A more valuable understanding develops in recognizing these reinforcing aspects of the DDR program and to then consider which area (disarmament or demobilization) one should emphasize to encourage success in the *overall* DDR project.

"Commanding" Demobilization and Removing Commanders

As the official definition states, demobilization requires the "formal and controlled discharge" of combatants. In more organized "regular" forces, the physical manifestations of this demobilization are easier to identify (the surrendering of uniforms and/or rank insignia especially). Demobilization requires the removal of combatants from the command structures of their groups whether a standing military or an irregular force. In the Timor case, for example, the pro-Indonesia militias were essentially an extension of the Indonesian armed forces. While this provided some clarity regarding command structures, it reinforced tensions between the Timorese and Indonesian governments. However, increasingly militias have been independent of any national military structure. In cases where the militias are extensions of or auxiliaries to standing military organizations, demobilization is likely easier to initiate, so long as actual command and control remains strong between the military and the militia. Should that structure be broken, depending on the military to command demobilization by the militias can be problematic as the militias are now acting independently. In Sierra Leone, for example, the government established a "Civil Defence Force" (CDF) as a local security force to aid the armed forces against the rebels. The CDF membership drew originally from the traditional warrior/hunter class known as *kamajors*, a status both granted by paramount chiefs and also a reflection of the individual's prowess as a warrior. As a fairly exclusive class, paramount chiefs would usually only choose one or two people to be *kamajors*. However, these numbers grew during the civil war, as the *kamajors* themselves began to expand by recruiting their own members. Early on, the government incorporated the *kamajors* into the CDF, and their effectiveness in repelling attacks from rebels gave them strong public legitimacy. However, this effectiveness was generally confined to their local/traditional areas, and as the CDF grew larger in size, both social (chiefly) or government controls on CDF members began to decline. Furthermore, the internal discipline of the CDF based on the pride of being a *kamajor* also deteriorated, and some members committed abuses against the population.[10] (Among other abuses, the CDF will engage in the use of child soldiers, though it will hardly be the only group to do so in Sierra Leone. The issue of child soldiers will be covered in detail further in this chapter.) As membership in the CDF grew, that expansion brought with it a decline in the "quality control" and the power of traditional command structures within the group.

Controlling the discharge of combatants requires a delicate sense of timing as to when the elimination of the command structures should occur. The fact that the initial phase of demobilization can benefit from relatively strong command structures is a small irony. Having commanders with the ability to bring their forces in for demobilization with relative confidence makes the early stages of entry a less uncertain process (on the side of the combatants, at least. The demobilizing organizations may still have other obstacles to overcome). Furthermore, assuming the commander is playing "fairly," a group brought in by a commander for demobilization should be easier to identify and categorize (what organization the unit is from), which benefits accurate record keeping. An orderly and structured demobilization process is certainly desirable, but at some point, the militarized command structures must be deemphasized, or the *mental* demobilization process will falter. Placing demobilizing combatants in a situation that reinforces militarized command structures is obviously counterproductive.

There are two significant caveats regarding the power of commanders to bring their forces in for demobilization. The first is the problem of commanders "cheating" the program. Because DDR programs understandably offer incentives for entry, there is the potential for noncombatants to enter in order to gain access to these benefits. In Liberia, Paes suggests that some commanders paid noncombatants to turn in weapons and enter demobilization programs. These individuals would then split the monetary reward with the commander.[11] Most troubling, many of these noncombatants may have been children. This phenomenon raises some doubt as to the reported numbers of child soldiers demobilized. The consequences of this deception go far beyond the monetary fraud involved. If the children entered into demobilization centers are not really combatants, then actual child soldiers are being deliberately kept away from opportunities to demobilize. (Sierra Leone child protection agencies suggest that rather than allowing them to demobilize, commanders are using child soldiers as cheap labor in rubber plantations and gold or diamond mines.)[12] Paes further argues a potential indicator of false claims in that about a quarter of the caseload registered as "Other" rather than being identified with any of the armed groups.[13]

The second problem is that what appears to be demobilization may only mean the combatants have renounced the use of violence in the pursuit of some cause. It does not necessarily mean that they (or their leaders) have renounced the use of violence to achieve other goals, specifically economic gain. In this case, military trappings may go away, but the command structures and/or personal loyalties may remain. While demobilization and the associated reduction in number and

size of armed groups contributes overall to a general atmosphere of peace, at the microlevel, individual ex-combatants may
find themselves in greater positions of personal insecurity.
Fighting and violence as a way to make a living may replace
fighting for a cause. Without an effective reinsertion/reintegra-
tion program to help provide nonviolent future opportunities,
many combatants may turn to crime, mercenary work, or perhaps other causes, whether at home or in neighboring states.
Extremely profitable illicit activities such as the drug trade can
provide powerful temptations for combatants to use their "talents" to make a living, especially when the earlier justifications
for the group's existence and practices have less credibility
due to changes by the government. This problem has risen
in Northern Ireland, where both Republican and Unionist
vigilante groups, previously viewed by their respective communities as part of "legitimate" (albeit brutal) practices of policing
internal community behavior, may now be losing some of that
credibility. This decline is in part due to reforms connected to
the ongoing peace process, but is also a consequence of the
increasing involvement by the vigilante groups in criminal
enterprises.[14] This highlights a tension within an organization
as governments implement reforms to address the grievances
of the population. Does the organization diminish in importance, or does it find other ways to perpetuate its existence? A
group's metamorphosis from (at least ostensibly) protecting a
community to preying on it exposes this tension in its starkest
terms.

In Colombia, the profits generated by the drug trade gath-
ered "recruits" from both the guerrilla forces looking to
overthrow the government *and* the citizen militias such as
the United Self-Defense Forces of Colombia (AUC) originally
raised to help the military combat the guerrillas. This ironic
new arrangement arose when reforms removed many of the
political reasons for violence, but did not necessarily provide

greater financial opportunities. Individuals, especially those in the "middle management" levels, saw their livelihoods being undermined. It is also the case that as time goes on and organizations grow, the loyalty of the individual to the goals of the organization (or to its cultural/traditional values) may not be as strong. Restrepo and Muggah note that over time the AUC acted more as a "franchising organization" for citizen militia groups, providing training and other support to separate "branches" across the country. This practice allowed for an expansion in membership but also provided the opportunity for drug cartels to penetrate the organization.[15] Just as with the CDF in Sierra Leone, the rapid numerical expansion of an effective armed group brought with it an associated decline in the quality and effectiveness of its membership.

The increase in other forms of violence in the aftermath of demobilization is something that bears watching. It will arise as a consequence of the breakdown in command and control from higher levels to smaller groups (the problem of "middle management" within armed groups discussed in the previous chapter). Any armed group that becomes more interested in financial gain rather than their original political goal will find its political legitimacy declining (thereby losing popular support and giving to the government a point for propaganda purposes), but may be less inclined to demobilize regardless of any political compromises from the government. The drug trade seems especially amenable to this "profit-over-politics" evolution. Beyond the earlier examples of Northern Ireland and the AUC, groups such as the FARC in Colombia and some groups in Afghanistan have also exhibited this transformation.

Mental Demobilization: War Fatigue

Demobilization, like disarmament, is easiest (at least on paper) to implement in a situation of defeat or surrender. In

cases of military stalemate, peace agreements may be tenu-
ous, and requirements for demobilization can be dangerous,
especially if one side views the agreement as significantly
unfair. However, a long period of perceived military stalemate
can have a more positive effect on making the parties more
amenable to a peace agreement and demobilization. The phenomenon is referred to as "war fatigue," where the parties
over time have become exhausted with fighting. (More critically, the parties are exhausted with the *lack of achievement* of
their objectives via military means.) In this situation, the parties may begin to look for alternative ways to end the conflict,
given that military solutions are not viable. Edward Luttwak
has argued provocatively for the idea that interventions by
third parties into conflicts may in fact be counterproductive
for the long-term establishment of peace between the adversarial groups. He argues that the intervention before the onset
of "war fatigue" means the parties have not exhausted their
energy and inclination towards violence, and they lack the
long-term experience of fighting to a standstill.[16] War fatigue
(or the lack thereof) is an explanatory factor for the success/
failure of many cases of demobilization. Alusala notes in his
survey of Central African cases the large number of ex-combatants who prefer demobilization. He puts forward many
explanations for this, but does not mention war fatigue.[17]
In Mozambique, most combatants preferred to be demobilized rather than join the new Mozambique Defense Force
(FADM). One reason for this reluctance was the view that
FADM was not an attractive or viable career option. In contrast, demobilization benefits were clear and tangible. Beyond
that "rational" calculation, Berman also argues that, for many,
the chance simply to stop fighting was enough for demobilization.[18] Synge agrees, arguing that in fact the frustration of
the soldiers and their desire to stop fighting was the major
limitation to the resurgence of conflict.[19] Southall notes in the

case of Burundi that, despite many reservations from competing parties over the peace agreement brokered in 2000,
the parties recognized that the people were desperate for the
end of conflict.[20] This encouraged parties to push to make an
imperfect agreement work, rather than trying to construct the
perfect agreement. The war fatigue phenomenon is not limited simply to African cases. War fatigue was a major factor in
bringing the Bougainville Revolutionary Army to the negotiation table with the Papua New Guinea government. Frequent
statements on the part of the combatants on both sides of the
Bougainville conflict point to the exhaustion after a decade of
fighting making the parties more amenable to negotiation.[21]

   In contrast, the lack of war fatigue coupled with the absence
of any decisive military victory by one side or the other
explains some of the problems in demobilizing the armed
groups in Rhodesia/Zimbabwe. Since none of the armed
groups were actually defeated militarily, many tensions
between the Zimbabwe African National Liberation Army
(ZANLA) and the Zimbabwe People's Revolutionary Army
(ZIPRA) remained unresolved entering into later phases of
the DDR and peacebuilding enterprise.[22] In another example,
the Communist Party-Nepal has contested the applicability of
DDR models by claiming their army has not been defeated
and that what is occurring today is only political negotiation,
not demobilization.[23] Such statements are obviously worry-
ing when considering the progress towards peace in Nepal.
Absent a decisive victory by one side, peace negotiations carry
the shadow that a group will decide they have more to gain by
reigniting the conflict. Negotiations may also be imperiled if
the "victorious" side views their advances being taken away
during peace talks.

Cantonment

Demobilized combatants have to be placed somewhere, if not for the beginning of reintegration, then at least for basic registration and perhaps the surrendering of weapons. The United Nations Department of Peacekeeping Operations 1999 Guide on DDR considers cantonment a "vital requirement" of the DDR process.[24] Cantonment can be handled in many different ways, but most require at least an accessible assembly point, if not a larger gathering (and holding) place. An effective cantonment program requires balancing adequate resources with good timing. Failure on either dimension can lead to a return to violence.

The construction, supply, and maintenance of cantonment sites will be the most visible aspect of demobilization. It is a physical sign that armed groups are willing to depart militarized command structures and negotiate a return to civilian life. It also represents a commitment by the government (usually with the help of outside states and agencies) to ease and assist the transition of combatants. If cantonment is not adequately resourced, they will be considered little more than prisons.[25] A resurgence of violence is almost inevitable if the atmosphere within a cantonment site is an oppressive one. On the other hand, the sites must be recognized as temporary. They cannot be equipped so well that those going through the process view staying at the site better than reentering civilian life. Established sites are stable (and therefore have a measure of predictability) but more expensive to maintain. "Mobile" cantonment sites, where combatants are told in advance to meet in a specified location for demobilization for a limited period of time, are less expensive to maintain, but combatants may miss the time the site is active and mobile sites do not assist in breaking command structures.

The planned (or promised) duration for cantonment is

also vitally important, though its actual length may not be as significant as the promises made for services and the provision of educational/vocational programs for ex-combatants. Demobilizing "on schedule" can lead to renewed violence if the combatants do not feel they have received the promised benefits but were in fact cut off at a specified due date. Extending cantonment because all demobilization benefits have not been provided is an approach that requires careful negotiation. In particular, the reasons for the delay must be transparently articulated, and even then, there is some potential for violence and protests from the combatants. The cantonment period for Mozambique was meant to be only 6 months, but in fact took over 16 months.[26] The delay raised serious tensions within the cantonment sites, as many feared they were simply being held captive. (Even here, the length of stay was less problematic than the *perception* that the government was not keeping its promises.) International assistance for demobilization programs must be extremely cognizant that they do not produce these types of delays, which means they must consider the availability of resources, expertise and political will in its implementing schedule.

Cantonment allows for the gathering of combatants and the beginning of demobilization. The issue is whether cantonment diminishes or reinforces the command structures within the armed groups. The bureaucratic issues of registration, the initial distribution of benefits, and entry into vocational or other training programs are a visible phenomenon, but demobilization is about the *psychological* break from the militarized mentality stemming from membership in an armed group. Knight and Özerdem consider cantonment's greatest contribution to DDR is in the area of child soldiers. Since many of these children have no community to return to (due to being forcibly taken and/or committing atrocities in their former community), they will need a place to stay before finding a new home. They argue that cantonment is the way to separate child soldiers from military authority and to protect them before beginning the reintegration process.[27] This works best, of course, in separate locations and with programs that will assist in the transition to civilian life. Özerdem suggests that planning for demobilization should examine issues addressing the future of individuals who will *not* become part of the new security structure.[28] Indeed, this is the central purpose of demobilization, as those individuals who do become part of the new security structure have been "remobilized."

Demobilization and Remobilization: The Reconstitution of a National Security Force

While most, if not all, members of an irregular force will demobilize during the post-conflict/peace process, at least a portion may return to the profession of arms as part of a newly constituted security force. There are several technical advantages to this reconstitution. Since not every member of the armed groups will join the new security force, there is an expected decline in future military expenditure with fewer soldiers.[29] Evidence from African cases suggests, however, that these savings do not come about very quickly and are not as high as predicted, so a demobilization process may succeed on a technical level but still cause social and financial issues.[30] In cases of "successful" insurgencies, the insurgent group simply reforms as the security force of the new nation. East Timor and Kosovo are good examples of this phenomenon, but even in these cases, not every member of the Falintil or the Kosovo Liberation Army became a member of the national security force.

The establishment or reconstitution of a new national security force may be "easy" in the aftermath of victory by one side, but the more difficult cases arise when formerly opposing groups and/or military forces must now come together as a security force for a shared state. The increasing number of parties with a stake in the potential composition of the new security force only exacerbates the complexity of the situation. In Rhodesia, not only did the militias fight against the Rhodesian Security Forces, but factions emerged among the militias themselves, leading to rivalry and conflict. Critically, since none of the armed groups was actually defeated militarily, no one side was willing to compromise. ZANLA considered itself the "victors" (they had, after all, achieved their political goal) and should take the lead in constituting the new nation's security force. In contrast, the Rhodesian Security Forces did not consider the "guerrillas" a viable nucleus for a standing military force (Ginifer notes that of all the groups, ZIPRA was the most helpful in developing guidelines and procedures for integration).[31] There is also the possibility that individual ex-combatants will choose not to join. Under the terms of the peace agreement, the government and the rebel forces would provide the personnel for the new Mozambique Defense Force (FADM). Rather than having too many people seeking to remain in the military, both sides were faced with too few.[32] (This situation also contributed to suspicion on both sides that combatants were being kept in reserve, suggesting that the respective rival groups were not truly serious about peace and societal reintegration.)

Berdal asks the very interesting question of *when* demobilization should occur in relation to the integration and establishment of the new national armed force. Most cases opt for demobilization before reconstitution, since it is much cheaper. As an advantage, Berdal points out that demobilizing after integration allows for a more accurate registration and survey of the combatants.[33] Furthermore, demobilizing after the development of a new security force allows for governments to consider the talents of all potential members. This assembling of combatants before demobilization took place in Mozambique. This was done to begin the integration of the FADM. However, since many combatants did not want to become part of the new integrated force, waiting for a greater number of assembled troops before initiating demobilization only served to increase the strain (both psychological and resource wise) on those already assembled.[34]

The political agreement to organize and integrate a national security force is one thing, but actually crafting a security force that integrates well internally while also being a proficient combat force is something else. Combat power is not only about the proficiency of troops, but encompasses a host of support and other logistical issues. At the organizational level, the varying skills (or lack thereof) from different groups can create unintended tensions. Guerrillas do not always make the best conventional fighters, and many do even worse in the more administrative functions of a formal military. The development of an integrated South African National Defence Force (SANDF) at the end of the apartheid regime highlighted these problems. South Africa is an interesting case, since arguably few societies were as significantly divided prior to the reconstitution of a new national security force. Despite that division, it achieved a full demobilization of combatants and reintegration of a national security force without external intervention. At the operational/implementation level, however, South Africa offers fewer transferable insights since it never lost its internal infrastructure or political authority to oversee the transition.[35] The "defeated" South African Defence Force in fact became the administrative and bureaucratic backbone of the new SANDF, due to its "virtual monopoly of the formal staff skills . . . and its familiarity with the . . . strategic and doctrinal issues underpinning both the planning and force design process."[36] This advantage in organizational prowess, when added to the sheer weight of numbers in the new SANDF (former SADF members were the overwhelming majority) had the consequence of marginalizing many non-SADF members from the new SANDF. While in most cases these structural biases are unintended, spoilers within the system can take advantage of the numerical advantage as well as superior bureaucratic prowess. The value of mid-level leaders is as critical here as it was in the disarmament phase. Their lack of support can allow them to inhibit the shift to an integrated security force without visible opposition.

In the final analysis, governments may simply have to ride out the storms inherent in reconstituting a new security force, recognizing these pains as inevitable to accomplish community peace. This is especially true in societies split along ethnic or other lines. Organizing armed forces into segregated units along ethnic or tribal lines will certainly be "easier" for the government to put in place, and doing so may even be justifiable for reasons of effectiveness (multilingual societies may find it more effective to group native speakers together), but this kind of segregation dilutes the development of an ethos of "national" identification. A security force that is professional and viewed as representative of (or at the very least, not viewed as a threat to) the larger society from which it comes can be a powerful symbol of national identity for ordinary citizens and establish a unifying identity within the security force. These larger reforms are generally beyond a strict DDR program, but are connected to it in via the practice of Security Sector Reform (SSR).

DDR and Security Sector Reform (SSR)

The design and establishment of a new security force should take place within a larger discussion of SSR. Bryden and Hänggi argue that "reconstruction" instead of "reform" may be a more accurate conceptualization for the processes involved here, since "reform" practices have drawn mostly from experiences with developing or post-authoritarian societies.[37] Current practices in post-conflict situations (like DDR) are often not part of the "reform" context. The reconstruction of the security sector, more importantly, must be tied to larger issues of governance.[38] This is evident in the reconstitution of the security force in Nepal. The Comprehensive Peace Agreement of 2006 between the government and the Maoist insurgents ended a decade-long conflict and signaled the end of a monarchy that ruled Nepal for over two centuries. Reforming and reconstituting the national security force is now occurring in the context of moving toward a republican form of government. However, the agreement, despite its title, has not been very "comprehensive," with the most difficult decisions being deferred to the future.[39] The former "Royal" Nepalese Army has always been viewed as serving the interests of the monarch, not the larger society.[40] The Maoists, despite the usual rhetoric of serving the "masses," have for the most part supported themselves. Neither institution has therefore been representative of the population, so this shift in identity will be critical in the development of a unifying identity within the security force.

Tying SSR to larger issues of governance means that not only must the military force be a reflection of the country and society it protects, the larger government itself must also be working in the interests of *all* of its citizens. This is easier said than done. The government as a belligerent actor involved in a conflict against a segment of its population will obviously not have the political capital to encourage the demobilization of irregular forces.[41] (Indeed, many of those groups will see themselves – and be seen by much of the larger populace – as the force protecting the population from the danger of oppressive government forces.) The perception (reinforced by actions) that the government is an honest broker attempting to balance the needs and interests of all segments of its population is a powerful aid in the road to post-conflict demobilization and subsequent reconciliation. The government's attempts at reforms are important to bring opposition groups (armed or otherwise) into political discourse, but the government must also be careful not to alienate its current support base. The problem becomes much more acute when the government is dealing not only with security sector reform and *improvements* in governance, but with a complete transformation of the government system. Most particularly, the transition from authoritarian rule to more democratic systems raises these tensions.

The "Dangers" of Democratization

While democratic nations are generally stable, countries that are in the midst of democratizing can find themselves in serious peril. Transitioning from authoritarian rule towards more democratic arrangements is always a precarious situation. The opening of political discourse and personal freedoms is an attempt by the government to ease into (and no doubt, control) a period of transition and change. However, this move can signal the regime's vulnerability to more impatient elements in the larger population. On the other side of the coin, reforms will inevitably upset the current elite. Even when the type and purpose of reforms are agreed upon, the time required for their implementation can be a matter of serious disagreement.

It is generally understood that insurgencies do not spring from nothing, and that the move towards armed violence is seen as a "last resort" of a frustrated segment of the population. Their grievances are not being addressed by the state. More critically, the group considers their inability to gain redress as illegitimate. They have not lost "fairly" in some process that took their voice into account, but are being disenfranchised without recourse. (Frustrations can arise even in systems and societies where *truly* fair processes constantly and consistently produce results where one identifiable side always loses, but this is a less frequent phenomenon.) By the time organized armed resistance is prevalent, the state's hold on the legitimate monopoly of violence is contested.

From the counterinsurgency perspective, it is also a well-understood tactic to undermine the insurgency by attempting to address some of the grievances that give it its emotional power. (There is certainly no small irony here. Had the government attempted to address these issues earlier, there would have been less need – and legitimacy – for the use of violence in the first place.) The problem with the government now attempting to compromise with the insurgent group is that the group may feel emboldened with its progress, and those already in support of the government may see such action as "rewarding" the insurgents for the use of violence.

Until 1988, governors in Colombia were appointed by the president. These governors then appointed the mayors within their regions. This system obviously centralized power and was one factor leading to armed conflict. Subsequent political reforms established open elections at these levels. This new system, however, opened the possibility that former "guerrillas" would become duly elected mayors and/or governors, making the old elite feel even more insecure and intransigent towards any other new reforms. These reforms are designed to bring the guerrillas into society, but drive more conservative elements of the society away from reconciliation. The military and regional elites are especially resistant to these overtures.

The case illustrates the danger in considering reforms as

universally accepted. Factions within the community can have different, even competing perceptions of the reforms. Even when the reform itself is understood, the idea that it was "achieved via illegitimate violence" can hinder its acceptance among other segments of the community. The time when governments open up and initiate reforms is an uncertain one for everyone involved. Governments seek to quell rebellion and answer grievances, but still hold power. Opposition groups, however, may sense weakness and demand greater reforms and/or the government's ouster. Balancing these tensions is the goal for every government seeking to lead reform, not be swept away by it.

Further Reading: Mauricio Romero, "Paramilitary Groups in Contemporary Colombia," in Diane Davis and Anthony Pereira, eds, *Irregular Armies and Their Role in Politics and State Formation* (Cambridge: Cambridge University Press, 2003).

Child and Women Combatants

The demobilization process is a traumatic one for all concerned. However, this situation is even more acute for child and women combatants. In the case of individuals who were brought (willingly or otherwise) into the force as children, a life of combat and the social practices of the armed group may be all that the individual knows or remembers. Breaking away from this network of relationships, even with the promise of peace, may be too uncertain for many to bear, leading many to revert and cling to familiar (albeit violent) patterns of behavior. Since many programs attempt to demobilize children as quickly as possible, this psychological shift is inevitably incomplete. Indeed, it is difficult to say how much time it takes for this shift to fully occur, or in fact if it ever does.

Properly identifying combatants is critical in implementing any demobilization program. Women and child combatants are usually disadvantaged in this situation (with girl members of the armed group being doubly disenfranchised). As mentioned previously, disarmament programs that require the surrender of a weapon are generally biased against women and children, many of whom have been part of "support" functions within the armed group and may not possess a personal weapon. Depending on what criteria are used for disarmament or demobilization, women and children may have weapons taken from them, or other symbols of combatant status forcibly removed by commanders for their own personal gain. Groups that are concerned with international opinion may simply be motivated to downplay the level of child soldiers within their organization. Obviously, women and children can still be connected to an armed group even if they did not engage in combat themselves, but this puts them in a different category than "combatants." This distinction may have value politically or economically (in terms of identification and distribution of financial assistance, for example), but it can also downplay the experience of conflict and its impact on everyone involved, whether or not they were actively engaged in fighting.

For female ex-combatants, the demobilization and return to civilian society can bring with it a greater sense of disorientation. Combat experience has generally been more easily reconciled with notions of masculinity, and female combatants can find it difficult to return to more traditional roles. Indeed, the fact that a woman may have been a combatant can lead to community shaming, and in many cases female combatants have simply chosen not to identify as combatants (thereby denying themselves access to demobilization benefits) rather than suffer condemnation. Some agencies view the general absence of women in the demobilization process as evidence of their "self-demobilization." While in some cases this may be true, the stigma placed on women combatants by the community clearly plays a role in their absence in official demobilization programs. The general assumption is that both the women and the community view combat as a negative experience, but in some cases, there is a different problem, as some women may not want to return to the old norms, as seen in Ethiopia.

The Stigma of Identification of Combatants (or Lack Thereof): *Women in Ethiopia*

The demobilization of women combatants in Ethiopia offers interesting insight into the problems faced by women in a post-conflict environment. The experiences reveal some obstacles that even the best-planned demobilization program cannot address adequately. It also illustrates the tension between governmental (public) goals and community (social) expectations. While governments (and the international community) strive to ensure as many combatants are as "properly" demobilized as possible, communities may wish to deny the presence of combatants (especially women and children), setting up a dilemma for many female combatants to either go through the demobilization process and be shunned or refuse to identify and lose tangible benefits.

The experience in Ethiopia suggests another side to the issue of stigmatization. There is a general assumption in practically the entire DDR project that the experience of war is a negative one for all concerned, but perhaps most acutely for women and child combatants. The violence and trauma of war are terrible without question, but some evidence suggests that the idea of a universally negative experience should be questioned. In the Ethiopian case, many former female combatants reflect on their experiences with less universal condemnation. Despite the violence and other hardships experienced, some interviewees viewed their time as a combatant as one where they learned certain skills, self-sufficiency, and where their opinions and ideas were valued by others (especially male combatants). This experience has made it difficult for some to return to more "traditional" feminine values.[42]

The dilemma is twofold for these women. On the one hand, the traditional values that they are to reintegrate into cause their experience as combatants to be devalued, if not outright condemned. This condemnation makes it difficult for these women to find husbands and reenter society as "suitable" women. (This disapproval can even come from male ex-combatants who may now be looking for a "proper" wife.) On the other hand, many of these women developed some elements of self-sufficiency during their time as combatants. They may in fact be unwilling in to return to those traditional ways (indeed, in some cases these values may have been part of what they were fighting against), and instead may view their time as soldiers to be the more positive experience.

There is no technical "fix" to this situation; it strikes at the heart of the demobilization and reintegration experience. While men also have to deal with notions of masculinity and its relationship to the use of violence, women have to balance receiving physical benefits from demobilization with the acceptance of the community. Programs focused on the needs of the community must give greater emphasis to this tension. More pointedly, while most programs understandably focus on helping former combatants adjust to returning to the community, some programs that educate the community about former combatants should receive greater consideration.

Further Reading: See Angela Veale, *From Child Soldier to Ex-Fighter: Female Fighters, Demobilisation, and Reintegration in Ethiopia*, Monograph 85 (Pretoria: Institute for Security Studies, 2003).

In cases like Ethiopia, the community is therefore also confronted with the situation that some former combatants may not, in fact, wish to reintegrate, or at least not on the terms that the larger community may have expected. This problem also arises in the demobilization of child soldiers. An unfortunate demographic logic drives the use of child soldiers in both irregular groups and standing militaries. Societies where the average overall life expectancy is low will have an increasing number of youth relative to the rest of the population. Given this demographic division, the motivation to draw from younger segments of the population as part of the armed force is tragically rational.[43] This demographic motivation is further encouraged by technological advances in weaponry. In particular, the reduction in size and weight of assault rifles has made it easier to put children into combat situations.[44]

Demobilization requires the breakdown of the command relationships of the armed groups. Effectively disconnecting combatants from commanders requires an understanding of the motivation of the recruits. Alfredson notes rightly that the distinction between voluntary and coercive recruitment is ambiguous.[45] It is better to understand the motivations for recruitment as a spectrum rather than binary categories, but certainly there are differences found at the extremes. Coercive recruitment techniques frequently involve the committing of atrocities against one's community. Committing such acts both binds the child combatant to the armed group and can literally eliminate any "home" community for potential return. First-person accounts of child soldier experiences, such as Ishmael Beah's, have greatly raised the visibility of the plight of child soldiers, though not without some controversy. Finally, the psychological scars for all concerned (as well as any understandable grudges on the part of any survivors) will make the reintegration of child combatants very difficult.

Memoirs of a Child Soldier: The Ishmael Beah Controversy

A Long Way Gone, a memoir of Ishmael Beah's experience as a child soldier in Sierra Leone, was published in 2007. In the book, Beah details two years (1993–1995) as a child soldier with the Sierra Leone military. He describes events such as his forced separation from his family, taking drugs before combat, witnessing the committing of atrocities, and various other violations of the laws of armed conflict. The book was an international bestseller (due in part to prominent advertisement and distribution in Starbuck's coffee houses) and raised significant awareness of the child soldier phenomenon.

In 2008, reporters from the newspaper *The Australian* raised questions as to the veracity of Beah's story. They argued that Beah could not have been a child soldier for the years he claimed, but in fact may have been a combatant for no more than two months. Regarding the events in the book, there were arguments that, while all of the events in the book certainly did happen in Sierra Leone, all of them happening to one person would be quite unlikely. Beah's editors (if not Beah himself) were accused of combining the experiences of several people into Beah's book. The fact that a few non-fiction books (such as James Frey's *A Million Little Pieces* about his experience as a drug addict) had been exposed just around this time for exaggerating time and/or events did not help Beah's case, and neither did his assertion of having a photographic memory about his experiences (giving him little room to admit to any possibility of mistake or exaggeration). Beah and his publishers have stood by his story. Others, while critical of Beah's possible exaggerations and use of poetic license, still credit the book with raising the important issue of child soldiers to a larger audience.

Further Reading: Ishmael Beah, *A Long Way Gone* (New York: Farrar, Straus, and Giroux, 2007) and Marcus Baram, "Does Best-Seller Bend the Facts?" ABC News, http://abc-news.go.com/US/story?id=4184154&page=1, January 25, 2008 (accessed February 10, 2010).

While there is increasing attention on the plight of child soldiers today, an invisible cohort of combatants who have "aged out" of being considered a "child combatant" remains, and their problems are no less dire if not more so. Child combatants are defined as those under the age of 18 years, and the international community (UNICEF in particular) has instituted several programs to aid in the transition of child soldiers back to civilian life. These programs, however, do not apply to individuals who are 18 years or older at the time of demobilization, even if these individuals were recruited as minors and spent the bulk of their youth as a combatant. Treated simply as adult combatants, these individuals currently fall through the cracks regarding any special demobilization programs or counseling. There is to date little specialized research on the special challenges faced by this cohort. Agencies should consider a special category for these individuals who have lost their childhood to armed conflict.

After Demobilization: The Uncertain Steps towards (Re)integration

The demobilization process should carry within it the basis of reintegration for the combatant into the post-conflict society.

In the new post-conflict era, the combatants must have hope for a peaceful community. There has to be a future *after* demobilization. Obviously, a major part of that hope must be some optimism for economic development.[46] This optimism is tied to at least some basic skills that could open doors for employment or other business opportunities. Connection and support of fellow ex-combatants is something that should be examined, with its beneficial aspects encouraged as much as possible. Synge notes in Mozambique that neither the veterans nor handicapped veterans organization received any international assistance.[47] These organizations are critical in the demobilization and reintegration of combatants and giving them support can help prevent the creation of "underground" networks of dissatisfied ex-combatants. This point, coupled with the fact that most of these veterans will still be quite young, again highlights the problem of successful demobilization and reintegration.

For children in the post-conflict environment (combatants or otherwise), hope for the future is tied not only to employment, but avenues for education. The problem of school fees can be a hindrance to getting an education, however. Verwimp and Verpooten note that in Rwanda's capital of Kigali, fees for secondary schools for one child was nearly equal to the demobilization payment to ex-FAR soldiers. This fee was paid by the government and via donor funds from 1995–2000 for children of murdered Tutsis, and others received assistance from the Ministry of Local Affairs. Children with living parents, though, had to pay their own school fees.[48]

The break from military life to the civilian world can be a disorienting, even traumatic, experience. The United States and most other developed countries have developed large programs to assist military personnel and their families in making that transition. The basic (and generally valid) assumption is that the social patterns and relationships in the civilian world are different from those in the military. However, what if the situation is, rather than an armed group being a new set of relationships, it is in fact a "traditional" social network that has been militarized? This is the fascinating argument put forward by Danny Hoffman in his analysis of testimony given by former CDF members in Sierra Leone. Hoffman argues that since the CDF draw their traditional legitimacy from earlier *kamajor* traditions, they should be considered a social network that has become militarized, rather than a "military organization."[49] As discussed earlier, the expansion of the CDF diluted many of these traditional relationships, so Hoffman's analysis should be somewhat tempered. For those individuals with deeper ties to the *kamajor* values, however, understanding the CDF as a militarized social network is extremely valuable, since it raises the (unfortunate) prospect of viewing war not as a replacement for "normal" relationships, but a militarizing of established social networks. This understanding raises different avenues and obstacles regarding the demobilization of different CDF members. If Hoffman is correct, then "standard" demobilization does not break the command structures of a militia because those structures are more than simply "military" ones, but have an older and deeper pedigree. "The patronage networks which dominate everyday existence have not been replaced in wartime, they have simply become militarized. Ex-combatants remain dependent on their commanders even after disarmament."[50]

A larger issue encompasses Hoffman's argument. Successful demobilization and reintegration programs must appeal to and undermine the combatants' motivation that led to his/her recruitment and retention. Emphasizing the technical aspects of DDR has kept the international community less equipped for understanding the motivations of combatants in specific contexts. Berdal notes the US assumption that many internal and regional conflicts (Angola, Cambodia,

Central America, and Mozambique, to name a few) were motivated largely by Cold War dynamics.[51] This overemphasis on the bipolar conflict obscured powerful underlying tensions that will shock an unprepared international community (Afghanistan, Central America, and Yugoslavia being only the most prominent examples). Bøås and Hatløy's research argues that the primary reason combatants joined armed groups in Liberia was security (rather than popular arguments that these young men joined due to "idleness" due to unemployment). Concerns over personal security required immediate attention and there was less potential for planning for the future without satisfying the security issue. If such is the case, then demobilization and reintegration programs that stress jobs placement, while certainly welcome, do not cut to the heart of the reason for their joining an armed goup.[52] They note accurately, "the trick for the Liberian government and the international community is to stabilise Liberian society sufficiently so that youth can finally begin to think strategically, not tactically."[53] Reducing the threat of organized, militarized violence is demobilization's central purpose; it eliminates the need to focus solely on tactical calculations of security. Establishing an environment that opens the ability for strategic thinking, not just among the youth, but for all segments of the population, that is the basis for reintegration.

CHAPTER FIVE

Reintegration: The End of the Beginning

The Critical Phase

There is little question that reintegration is the most important phase of the DDR project. It is the point where everything
comes together, placing the former combatants and the larger
community on the path to long-term peace. Reintegration is
"the process by which ex-combatants acquire civilian status
and gain sustainable employment and income. Reintegration
is essentially a social and economic process with an open
time frame."[1] Due partly to this more undefined time frame,
the effectiveness of the reintegration phase is more difficult
to assess than disarmament or demobilization.[2] Regardless
of how effective disarmament and demobilization may be,
they are at best only a symptom of movement towards societal reconciliation. The reduction of weapons in an area may
not increase the community's sense of safety. Demobilization
only works if the communities perceive the security situation as improved to the point that self-defense forces are no
longer necessary or legitimate. While some combatants will
continue to use violence for other reasons (such as criminal
profiteering), demobilization can be considered a success if
such violence is viewed as illegitimate and the government
security forces are viewed as the proper institution to address
the situation. This perception of the government forces is
influenced by many factors, such as their composition and
their actual effectiveness in keeping the population safe, but

the very perception of their legitimacy also gives them some leeway regarding their institutional effectiveness. The rise of criminal activity by "demobilized" members of armed groups may not necessarily equal the failure of the demobilization project. Pozhidaev and Andzhelich list several positive and negative factors for reintegration,[3] but the significant question is one of perception, especially the difference between international community (outsiders) and the affected domestic community (insiders). It is *always* the insider perceptions that determine the ultimate value of the DDR project. Regardless of how much progress international agencies or other governments assess (or assert) is occurring, without the affected community believing that advances are happening, there is no meaningful measure of success.

Despite the clear recognition of the importance of reintegration, it is also frequently the least funded in the DDR process. Because it takes so long, and likely because it occurs so much later in the peace process, the international community loses interest in the project. Despite the early recognition that reintegration was necessary in Kosovo, for example, international funding for reintegration programs was quickly phased out.[4] The IDDRS recognizes reintegration as a national responsibility, but one that will usually require outside assistance.[5] This decrease of attention by the international community during the reintegration phase places an even greater onus on the national government and domestic community to address reintegration issues via their own resources, and to plan for just such a contingency. This is not just in the area of economics, where the reality is that resources will always be inadequate, even with outside assistance. More importantly, the national government and local communities are responsible for the social and psychological reintegration of former combatants and the society. Since it is the perception of the insiders that ultimately determines the success of DDR, their efforts are what matter for the success of establishing long-term peace, regardless of the support (or lack thereof) from international actors. As Furley and May note accurately, "durable solutions lie not in external interventions, but in internal transformation."[6] While reintegration has both subjective (how the ex-combatant sees his/her reintegration progressing) and objective (what programs the society is actually implementing) measures,[7] it is the subjective measures that are the more valuable indicator of progress. Just as the number of weapons collected during the disarmament phase is less important than building an atmosphere of trust and the psychological shifts by ex-combatants, so too are the individual and community perceptions more important than objective measures such as, for example, the number of former combatants in vocational programs.

Reintegration into What?

The entire DDR process moving towards reintegration stresses the physical, psychological, and social shifts from "combatant" to "civilian," but this is not simply an internal or individual process. While reintegration focuses on the internal issues of the combatants, there has to be an external context that encourages and reinforces these changes. Reintegration is the process of internal change within a new external context. Jennings points out that asking this larger question of "reintegration into what?" shifts the focus from the individual to the community.[8] This shift leads to an important framework for considering former combatants. The point is to develop their identity not simply as "civilians," but to a greater extent develop a communal identity of being a "citizen." This centers around the requirement for a meaningful social contract between the government and individual regarding what is expected from one and obligated to the other. Achieving a fair and realistic balance in this relationship between the citizen and the state is a true representation of a "reintegrated" society. It is also far beyond the scope of most theoretical and political understandings of what "reintegration" within the DDR program entails. However, the DDR project needs to recognize the concept of an effective citizen–state relationship to enable practitioners to track trends in improvement.

The open-ended understanding of reintegration makes achieving agreement on appropriate measures of progress and time frame extremely difficult. This is not just true between the affected community and the outside agencies, but within those groups as well. This vagueness has some political benefit, as it allows groups to work together without having to make some difficult decisions about agreed goals, but it also creates a situation where the program can be criticized for a lack of clarity of mutual understanding.

Types of Reintegration

Kingma distinguishes between different types of reintegration: political, social, and economic.[9] "Successful" reintegration has to encompass all of these dimensions, at least to some degree. There need to be arrangements (usually a peace agreement) that either address the political disagreements between the groups or at minimum set up a tentative framework for negotiations on these disagreements to occur. This macrolevel discussion may also require negotiations with neighboring countries on several issues. In terms of land issues, there may be a discussion on a new international border, especially in the case of a successful separatist movement. There may be other land reform issues, such as the provision of patches of land for returning combatants. Governments will also have to address the repatriation of individuals who have either fled the conflict from one side or entered into it from the other. Whatever the final *official* agreements on the placement of combatants are, the relationship between ex-combatant and community will take time to develop towards reconciliation. Finally, a war-torn economy must be revitalized. This must first occur at the community level to insure the security of the community, but must extend to the national and international arenas as well.

The social reintegration of combatants generally implies that there is a society, a community, available for return of former combatants. That society is often assumed to be the *status quo ante*, but this is a simplistic understanding of the problem. Gamba notes succinctly, "It has been customary for international and governmental agencies assisting in the process of demobilization and reintegration to look at this issue as if it were a minor correction rather than a major overhaul of society."[10] Any society touched by conflict has been changed significantly, and returning to a utopian vision of the past is impossible. Reintegration cannot just mean reintegration into the previous society, but about creating an atmosphere or process where disagreements and grievances are addressed without violence or the chronic threat of violence. In short, effective reintegration occurs within the larger context of post-conflict reconciliation and reflects the development of a meaningful relationship between the citizen and the state.

At its most basic level, this citizen–state relationship is one where the use of violence as a means to redress grievances is less likely than other measures. As Kingma writes, successful peacebuilding is where "the security vacuum that both state and non-state actors try to fill by violent means needs to be filled by legitimate political structures."[11] Specifically, this requires a system where the system to redress grievances are legitimated by *and* also legitimate the state. This means that reintegration programs have to consider both national-level agreements and (perhaps even more significantly) community-level programs and make sure these systems reinforce each other.

If the reintegration programs include assistance and/or mediation by outside organizations (other governments, especially), then these considerations are much more difficult to address. State-to-state relations are embodied in treaties, and while peace agreements and other programs may address problems at the macrolevel, they are less capable (or simply meaningless) in addressing tensions at the community-level. On the other hand, recognizing the need for reconciliation at national or community levels may be problematic for outside actors. For effective social reintegration in Afghanistan, for example, arrangements must be made that bring at least some elements of the Taliban to the negotiating table. However, the idea of some kind of rapprochement with Taliban elements (especially those with clear ties to Al Qaeda) will be unpalatable for the United States and other international partners. There is frequently disagreement in prioritizing threats and considering negotiations with sub-state actors between many national governments and international partners. In Southeast Asia, countries such as Indonesia and the Philippines have often disagreed with international partners on this matter. The Jarkarta government, especially the military, has been more concerned with separatist movements in Aceh rather than transnational organizations like Jemaah Islamiyah. The successful separation of Timor Leste in 1999 only exacerbated this concern.[12] Intriguingly, in April 2010 the International Crisis Group issued a report about the discovery and breakup of a militant Islamist organization in Aceh (a group that splintered from Jemaah Islamiyah, viewing the latter as too weak). The critical early insight was that very few members of this group had strong ties to the long-standing Free Aceh Movement (GAM). This suggest that ongoing efforts for the reintegration of GAM members are showing some success, but also highlights the need for greater vigilance, as different groups (targeting different grievances or disagreeing on the level of compromise with the government) can rise and transform the type of political violence.[13] It also means a need for greater precision in analysis, as increasing violence can either mean the splintering of the main groups (more intransigent elements refuse compromise and become more violent) or the rise of new groups (tied to different goals and grievances). Analysts must recognize these differences, as they speak to different motivations for violence and therefore different approaches to alleviating that violence. For the Philippines, the threat of the Communist Party-New People's Army generally looms larger than separatist and transnational movements in the Southern region. The Kabul government recognizes it has little choice but to achieve some kind of reconciliation with Taliban elements, and in fact the connection between the Taliban and transnational organizations is a lower priority for Kabul. In contrast, international partners are clearly more concerned with the connection between Taliban elements and transnational organizations, and certainly for the Western nations, the physical distance from Afghanistan also reinforces the luxury of intransigence regarding negotiations.

Community-level processes are often the most important for actually establishing post-conflict peace. Unfortunately, they usually do not get the visibility (or the associated funding) of national programs. Somewhat ironically, the ostensible target of reintegration programs is frequently the microlevel – the individual – but this is often disconnected from the needs of the community. Muggah points out that successful DDR programs are those perceived as benefiting entire communities rather than individuals.[14] The symbiotic relationship between individual combatants and the larger community for effective reintegration is often given little consideration.

This is especially evident in vocational or other economic programs, where the focus is on "job training," but this does not invariably lead to "job creation," and it is the latter that is truly important. Reintegration is not enabled by jobs that do not exist. In some cases, demobilization and reintegration will actually create *unemployment*, particularly among women. This phenomenon is frequently found in the demobilization of formal militaries at the end of a war. Women who have been working in "men's" jobs during wartime are no longer needed when men return from the battlefield. Developed nations dealing with these returning workers generally have economies robust enough to handle this influx, especially when the conflict takes place far from the nation's borders. In developing nations emerging from conflict, the economic consequences of a surplus of male workers is even more acute. However, for a variety of reasons, many women may have no choice but to remain within the wage-earning workforce. (An obvious situation is when women have lost their husbands or male relatives in the conflict.) With the returning males now in competition for jobs, women are either disenfranchised completely or compete by accepting lower salaries. In cases like Eritrea, women are pressured to return to the home in an effort to reduce male unemployment.[15]

Reintegration programs are generally more successful where there are networks of support (social and economic) that serve as alternatives to the armed group. Frequently, these alternatives require the revitalization of communal (in particular, kinship) relationships. Certainly, these structures can have great power in reestablishing peaceful post-conflict relationships. There were fears of a resurgence of violence in Mozambique after the last demobilization payment was disbursed. This did not happen, and Kingma argues that this was due to the fact that families and communities had already provided meaningful reintegration support.[16] Özerdem suggests that despite the lack of outside assistance, communities dealt with reintegration issues for the very pragmatic reason that they were tired of the conflict (the "war fatigue" phenomenon).[17] In cases such as Kosovo and Afghanistan, it was also relatively easy for members to return "home." This meant that little concern was given to "reintegration" in these areas, since the perception was the fighters had in fact already been reintegrated. This is partially true. The fighters returned to their communities, but the issue is the "community" in question. Kosovo and Afghanistan are arguably on opposite ends of the spectrum in the strength of a "national" identity. A robust national identity has been much easier to achieve in Kosovo (there are issues with new minority groups, but for the most part the "community" in Kosovo and its "national identity" overlap), but the very weak sense of national identity in Afghanistan remains a problem for future conflict. The ability to return is also conditioned by the current status of that community. Neither the community nor the individual combatant is a static entity, and the changes incurred during conflict will have serious ramifications for the ease of reintegration. Obviously, the trauma associated with atrocities shatter any previously held community relationships, creating significant obstacles to subsequent attempts at reintegration. In fact, Humphreys and Weinstein suggest the strongest predictor of difficulty to reintegrate is whether the combatant is associated with an armed group that abused civilians.[18]

Benefits notwithstanding, there are issues with these networks of identity. The most notable drawback to these tightly bonded, highly loyal community groups is their significant role in the development of organized crime.[19] This threat is especially likely in areas where illicit trade is already a profitable endeavor (such as drug trade, but this is true generally of more comprehensive smuggling operations). The previous chapter noted that the increasing involvement of irregular forces (whether formerly anti- or pro-government) in organized crime can reinforce command structures, but also make their intra-communal legitimacy problematic.[20] The rise of organized crime and an underground economic system is certainly a problem, but it may be a situation less threatening to the political stability of the government and the state more generally. For governments that have previously dealt with an armed insurgency, the recognition of a level of illicit economic activity without an associated political statement is almost a "palatable" problem, or at least provides a situation where the larger population recognize the government cannot deal with a problem "perfectly." This perception may give governments some "breathing space" to deal with this criminal problem without more pervasive political concerns. (The notion of "acceptable levels of failure" is discussed in the concluding chapter.)

The economic dimensions of reintegration are critical in moving ex-combatants into the civilian community. There is certainly a need to consider combatants as an important segment of society, one that require special consideration during peacebuilding. Most obviously, combatants are potential spoilers, with the ability to disrupt the fragile peace process through a return to armed violence.[21] To mitigate this potential threat, combatants must have some vision for their future economic livelihood that does not include the use of violence. However, while recognizing the spoiler potential of the combatants, reintegration benefits cannot be given as "entitlements" for the wartime experience or, even worse, seen as "rewards" for these prior acts of violence. The perception that reintegration incentives validate those past violent acts cripples the effectiveness of the program. An incentive structure that benefits "early demobilizers," however, has economic and political drawbacks. Economically, it will use most of its funding early, while offering the best deal at the outset does not leave any negotiating space to deal with the more reluctant combatants. More economically and politically sensible incentive structures also have their drawbacks. They increase the potential for hostility from the larger community toward the individual combatant, and can even increase resentment among former combatants who "choose peace" earlier. In Mozambique, added economic and other benefits encouraged increased demobilization in 1994. Those combatants who had demobilized the year prior (referred to as "the sixteen thousand") demanded they receive the same benefits as those who were now demobilizing.[22] In El Salvador, financial constraints required the government to exclude members of the civil defense groups as well as military personnel who were discharged prior to the end of the conflict from the severance pay package, causing understandable resentment.[23] In other cases, payments for demobilized irregular group members and those in the military were not equal, and while there are justifiable reasons for this, governments and other agencies have to consider the backlash that this practice can create. Reintegration benefits for former combatants must be developed along parallel and reinforcing paths as the former combatants' investment back into the community. Reintegration cannot be rewards for past action, but investments for future behavior.

Even in well-developed and stable economies, starting and maintaining a small business is very difficult. Many reintegration programs include employment assistance and vocational training for ex-combatants to give them a skill and return to the community. While combatants with experience in a particular business prior to the outbreak of conflict on their return to civilian life usually did better than those learning new skills, many ex-combatants struggled for a variety of reasons. Many of the programs produced an initial surplus (carpenters, mechanics, small grocery stores, etc.) in the immediate area. In some cases, individuals had to move away from their home regions (many just returned as part of the demobilization and reintegration package). Some of these individuals migrated to urban areas, increasing the strain on services there. In other cases, the training or tools provided were less than adequate for them to make a living. Finally, there is the unfortunate reality that not everyone will be a successful business owner. No reintegration program can address all of these issues, but a greater appreciation of the needs of the community would allow for more effective application of resources in training and educating ex-combatants to reinsert themselves into those gaps.[24] The perceived failure of the vocational programs certainly contributed to the disappointment of many ex-combatants. While a great deal of this disappointment can be attributed to unrealistic expectations of immediate profit and success, these employment programs focused mostly on technical skills and did little to help manage the expectations of those going through the program. Undoubtedly a byproduct of the lack of attention the reintegration phase generally has from the international community, the effective monitoring and follow-up on reintegration programs has generally been ignored. Research into the vocational programs in Rwanda illustrate this problem, as "no official was able to tell us whether the demobilized soldiers who received training were able to find a job later on or not."[25] Without any effective assessment, further assistance programs (whether domestically or internationally funded) will either be wasted or, even worse, allow corrupt officials to steal the funds with impunity.

Any successful economic reintegration must take into account the economic realities of the market within the immediate community and the larger nation. Many of these projects have failed due to a combination of unrealistic expectations of the recipients and inaccurate assessments by the government and/or international agencies on the economic outlook of the region. Communication and cooperation between national governments and international agencies (as well as between international agencies) need improvement, but the most significant shortcoming in economic reintegration has been the failure to effectively engage the private sector. Effective job creation is more than just the training of a pool of workers. Training all combatants is a single set of skills produces an immediate oversupply. Communication with the private sector can produce a better picture of the needs of the immediate community and also encourage a wider diversity of reintegration options.[26] This sets the groundwork for a more robust domestic economy and enhances the desire of former combatants to reintegrate and the resilience of the community to assimilate them socially and economically.

The ultimate goal of economic reintegration is to place the ex-combatant in a situation where he/she has the hope of a legal livelihood separated from armed violence (the slight exception being employment in the government security forces). This livelihood must be connected to the needs of the community, but it is not necessarily tied to the market. In more rural areas, giving ex-combatants training in subsistence agriculture (or other related skills, such as fishing or animal husbandry) is a beneficial skill in addition to whatever vocational training provided. Even in urban areas, if there are pieces of land sufficient for small vegetable farms, these should be encouraged. Rather than small vegetable gardens for each household, some areas may consider a communal garden. This will provide benefits not just due to the crops provided, but for the development of a community identity and strengthening the relationships between civilians and former combatants.

Everyone in the post-conflict community, whether civilian or former combatant, must confront the social and psychological issues and come to terms with the experience of the conflict and find ways to accept the past while building new relationships for the future. Reintegration requires coming to terms with the often horrific deeds perpetrated during the conflict and the roles and responsibilities of the individuals (and groups) that committed them. Two different problems of reintegration will be discussed here. The first is the reintegration of child soldiers, an act deliberately chosen by both "informal" armed groups and also by formal military organizations. The second problem is how to address irregular forces in the DDR program who, rather than fighting against the government of the day, in fact fight in support of it. Should that support accord members of these groups a different status or experience for DDR? The child soldier problem is described here as a "sin of commission," a deliberate act by an armed group that the group would prefer was ignored. The issue of pro-government militias is the government's "sin of omission," as these militias may expect a different level of treatment or reward than the government may be willing to give.

Sins of Commission: The Problem of Child Combatants

The reintegration stage is the point where the myriad offenses (real and imagined) of every group are confronted. It is at this stage, when there is some political and emotional space to have these discussions, that the groups must deal with the consequences of deviations from what are generally viewed as "acceptable" rules of armed conflict. This includes the perceived "honor" with which the conflict was fought, the amount and level of any atrocities committed, and finally whether those atrocities can be considered the "standard practice" of the armed group in question rather than the actions of rogue elements in the group. While the latter situation still calls for reconciliation at the individual level, the former requires a more comprehensive approach to address the issue.

Specifically, an armed group that has regularly used child soldiers has a significant "legitimacy gap" to overcome if it hopes to enter mainstream politics (or simply to achieve forgiveness) in the post-conflict society. This is only the initial (and relatively minor) aspect of the problem. The more significant issue is how to handle the reintegration of the child combatants themselves. Although recruitment of child soldiers may have been coerced, the reality that many child combatants committed atrocities against their own communities cannot be avoided. Reintegration programs frequently (and generally correctly) center around the trauma of the child combatant and focus on the need to prepare the child for eventual placement within a community. However, reintegration programs have been less attentive to the need to prepare the community for accepting the children. The idea that children are not as responsible for acts committed during the conflict may be understandable in theory, but the psychological scars on both the children and the community will not simply vanish with that theoretical understanding. As noted earlier, the strongest predictor of ease of reintegration is whether the individual was part of a group that committed atrocities against civilians. This context does not change if the former combatant is a child, and in fact it makes the reintegration experience that much more difficult. The issue of punishment and reconciliation is discussed later in this chapter.

The gender dimension adds another level of complexity to reintegration for girls. Those who have been brought in as "camp wives" or followers face additional obstacles for reintegration. Stereotypes of the feminine are still strong, and the stigma attached to the use of child soldiers is increased for many when it is girls who are used. Despite their connection to an armed group, they may not be considered "combatants" for the purposes of demobilization or reintegration benefits. Even if they have been combatants, they are the most likely (followed by boys) to have their weapons taken from them by their commanders, thereby losing their means of identification. Other factors mentioned earlier regarding adult female combatants and the possible reasons for their reluctance to identify as combatants also apply here, but this still means that these individuals are not assessed and many of their experiences are not recorded. Thus, they are frequently invisible in the discussions on reintegration programs.

After demobilization and psychological counseling, the former child soldier must have access to education. This is always difficult in the immediate aftermath of conflict. While this is sometimes due to the destruction of infrastructure, schools are in many ways one of the easiest projects for reestablishment. The more difficult problem is the provision of equipment and, more critically, qualified teachers. Teachers, and intellectuals more generally, either have fled areas of conflict or are likely dead, as the intellectual cohort is frequently a popular target in internecine conflicts. This lack of sufficient human capital for education is not as visible a problem as the lack of school buildings or supplies, but it is this limitation that will have greater ramifications for generations to come.

Sins of Omission: The Problem of Pro-Government Armed Groups

Irregular groups that attack the government in power and seek either its complete overthrow or some major shift in policy can easily be labeled "insurgents" or "rebels" by the government itself. In considering DDR programs for these groups, issues of trust are obvious and significant. Having fought against the government, ex-combatants must now be able to trust that there will be no reprisals and official security forces will in fact provide that community security. However, what is to be expected of militia groups that fought in support of, or were, in fact, established or supplied by, the government? What should be their expectations on DDR? Most importantly, what should be the expectations of the ex-combatants and the community at large regarding abuses committed by these individuals while serving in a pro-government militia? These latter questions can be especially problematic if not only the militias are on the "winning" side, but also the political "narrative" of the conflict ascribes a significant contribution to the militia for the "victory." Khokar's analysis of DDR and pro-government militias suggest that militias demobilizing with "friendly" governments find it easier to come to the negotiating table, but the DDR process itself is not any easier than for other armed groups.[27] Indeed, in some ways governments have even greater obstacles as these militias either may resent being treated as a "threat" or may feel a sense of entitlement for some reward or recognition for their contribution to the government's "victory."

The state's central dilemma in using or supporting civilian militias is that their very effectiveness can be problematic for the state. Local militias can be extremely effective in establishing political authority within a contested area. They are usually better in tune with local conditions than the larger government, and this situational awareness can help the local militia mitigate threats within its area. However, if these militias draw on other sources of authority apart from state sanction (and frequently they do), then the militia's power and ability also implicitly undermine the state's authority. This was the case in Sierra Leone (and peace accords made no mention of the CDF/*kamajors*).[28] In Afghanistan, many militias (known to the popular press as "warlords") sided with the international coalition against the Taliban to legitimize their standing.[29] The DDR process in Afghanistan is officially over and it is doubtful that any of these groups will be placed under any large-scale demobilization project anytime in the near future.

The reintegration phase in DDR is not the end of the peace-building process. At the very least, though, reintegration should bring some sense of closure to the conflict. Tensions may remain, but violence is not the expected form of redress. In some cases, this question of closure can have more than domestic implications. The supply and support of Indonesian militias by the Indonesian military in East Timor during the latter's struggle for independence has made that already strained relationship even more difficult for both govern-ments. In Kosovo, political separation from Serbia does not change the geographic connection between the two states.

Reintegration Into Where? The Dilemma for Successful Separatist Movements

Most contemporary conflicts have been intrastate situa-tions. Most of these conflicts have ended with the need for a reconciliation process to bring together armed groups *within* a single country. Very few modern conflicts have concluded with the creation of a new state. In such cases, reconciliation needs to give more attention to the inter-national ramifications and dimensions involved. While these issues are more about state-to-state relations than between individuals, the intentions of the DDR project are to encourage the conditions for long-term peace and recon-ciliation, and geopolitical relations clearly are an issue for consideration.

Certainly, all DDR projects have regional ramifications and need to consider their impacts on neighboring states. DDR can produce markets for weapons from neighbor-ing states, or combatants may cross borders to escape punishment or continue fighting, this time as mercenar-ies in a different conflict. These potential issues should be expected; no DDR project occurs in a vacuum. However, the situation of a successful separatist movement and creation of a new state creates dynamics arguably even more complex than those mentioned above. The recent cases of East Timor and Kosovo raise examples of successful internal reintegration but with problems at regional levels.

The breakaway of East Timor (Timor Leste) from the rest of Indonesia and Kosovo's separation from Serbia after the breakup of Yugoslavia offer recent examples of the establishment of new states and the subsequent demobilization and reintegration of their combat forces (the Falintil and the Kosovo Liberation Army (KLA), respectively). These cases also highlight the contributions that geopolitical tensions can have for societal and regional reintegration. Few countries are truly homogeneous, and should a separatist movement succeed, a group that had been a minority in a larger state now finds itself the majority in a smaller one (with a new "minority" group within its borders). These new social (and power) relations form the expanded context for community reintegration.

East Timor's referendum calling for independence from Indonesia was the result of a decades-long struggle for the Timorese population. Absorbed into Indonesia in the 1960s, the Timor population had long struggled to gain independence from its larger neighbor. Efforts by the Indonesian government to offer internal autonomy while holding Timor within the Indonesian state were refused, and the 1999 referendum overwhelmingly chose independence. Subsequent celebrations of the result included incidents of violence, and the Indonesian military entered to quell this disorder. Indonesians living in the Timor area formed self-defense militias to protect themselves. (Many of these groups were started and sponsored by the Indonesian military to stir dissent within Timor and to stir the population in the rest of Indonesia to support the government in holding East Timor by whatever means necessary.) The rising violence within Timor finally inspired an Australian-led intervention and subsequent UN administration. Timor Leste was finally independent in 2002.

After the breakdown of the former Republic of Yugoslavia, the Albanian-majority area of Kosovo attempted to secede from larger Serbia. Kosovo's 1990 declaration of independence received no international support (neighboring Albania was the only exception). Armed conflict between Serbian forces and members of the KLA was intense, and the North Atlantic Treaty Organization (NATO) announced in 1999 that it would intervene if the conflict did not end. Peace talks failed and NATO conducted a significant bombing campaign. Serbia's Slobodan Milosevic finally acceded to putting Kosovo under UN administration in 1999. Kosovo's successful separation from Serbia (with international intervention) also left northern areas of Kosovo that have rejected integration with the rest of the new state. Pristina's control over this northern area is minimal.

While both Falintil and the KLA contributed to achieving independence, both Timor Leste and Kosovo now have to face the geopolitical realities of being politically independent but still geographically (and economically) tied to a larger state. Timor Leste may eventually find greater economic stability due to its natural gas reserves, but as of 2011 remains one of the world's poorest states. Economically, Kosovo remains a ward of the international community. In both cases, the break from a larger state and separate ethnic group is not absolute. Some ethnic Indonesians remain in Timor, and negotiations for their "repatriation" to Indonesia continue. There are also still disagreements as to the border, though tensions have certainly lessened over the last few years. In the region of North Kosovo, Serbs are actually the numerical majority, and strong economic relations (including the funding of government services for the Serb population in North Kosovo) remain with the Belgrade government. These larger international tensions will influence internal reintegration in both states.

Further Reading: For Kosovo, see "North Kosovo: Dual Sovereignty in Practice," Europe Report 211 (Brussels: International Crisis Group, March 14, 2011). For Timor Leste, see Lars Waldorf, "Ex-Combatants and Truth Commissions," in Ana Cutter Patel, Pablo De Greiff, and Lars Waldorf, eds, *Disarming the Past: Transitional Justice and Ex-Combatants* (New York: Social Science Research Commission, 2009), and "Timor Leste: Oecusse and the Indonesian Border," Asia Report 104 (Dili and Brussels: International Crisis Group, May 20, 2010).

The Kosovo and Timor cases highlight the issue of regional DDR impacts, but nowhere is this situation more problematic than in the Great Lakes region of Africa. The World Bank, in coordination with the countries involved, established the most ambitious regional program for demobilization and reintegration – the Multi-Country Disarmament and Reintegration Program (MDRP).

Regional Arrangements for DDR: The Multi-Country Demobilization and Reintegration Program

Spillover effects are one of the most difficult problems affecting the entire DDR process. Geographic and political realities (ease of transit and sympathetic communities across borders are just some examples) require consideration to prevent the expansion or extension of a conflict. Spillover effects from disarmament relate to gun markets (prices) and the flow of arms. The regional impacts of

demobilization and reintegration can be even more complex, as repatriated ex-combatants may be "returned" to
areas that they have no loyalty for, thereby hindering prospects for reintegration. The Multi-Country Demobilization
and Reintegration Program (MDRP) is so far the most
ambitious attempt to deal with DDR and its impacts on
an entire region. The MDRP attempted to mitigate these
problems deriving from conflict in the Great Lakes Region
of Africa. In The MDRP addressed DDR issues in Angola,
Burundi, Central African Republic, Democratic Republic
of Congo, Republic of Congo, Rwanda, and Uganda. The
MDRP was the largst project of its kind. Establishing and
maintaining a program to harmonize DDR in seven different countries simultaneously had never been done before,
but the geographic and political realities meant that such
an approach would best minimize the possibility of negative spillovers.

The MDRP was initiated in April 2002 and closed in
June 2009. It was coordinated by the World Bank and
the major donors to the Program were Belgium, Canada,
Denmark, the European Union, France, Germany,
Italy, the Netherlands, Norway, Sweden, and the United
Kingdom. As its name might suggest, the MDRP did
not fund disarmament in the region, but rather focused
on demilitarization and reintegration projects for ex-
combatants. (The MDRP did have partner organizations
that were carrying out disarmament.) At its close, the
MDRP had contributed to the demobilization and reintegration of approximately 350,000 ex-combatants, at a cost
of US$560 million. Of that, just over US$250 million was
used to establish a Multi-Country Trust Fund to support
reintegration activities.

In in its final report, the World Bank highlights the value
of harmonizing contributions and activities by donors

and encouraging, wherever possible, host government and local ownership. The report stresses the value of local ownership while also acknowledging the significant risk involved if the host government is not capable of managing the process. Another insight from the report raises the consideration of separating DDR into two distinct phases – disarmament, demobilization, and short-term reinsertion as one phase, and longer-term reintegration processes as the second phase. Importantly, the closure of the MDRP does not mean the end of reintegration programs and assistance in the Great Lakes Region, as a smaller Transitional Demobilization and Reintegration Program is funded and expected to run from 2009 to 2012.

Further Reading: The World Bank, *MDRP Final Report: Overview of Program Achievements* (Washington, DC: The World Bank, 2010), and Scanteam, *Multi-Country Demobilization and Reintegration Program: End of Program Evaluation* (Oslo: Scanteam, 2010).

Reconciliation and Reintegration: Finding and Giving Forgiveness

The psychological trauma inflicted by conflict is rarely addressed completely. Kingma notes accurately "the confidence and security perceptions of citizens including ex-combatants is also affected by how past and ongoing human rights violations of members are handled."[30] Several nations and regions, varying from East Timor to South Africa and Northern Ireland have used "Truth Commissions" as a venue allowing combatants to express wrongdoing and for communities to express their anger, with an expectation that these expressions will move the parties toward reconciliation. Waldorf argues that the disconnect of DDR processes from truth commissions is a missed opportunity, as the reintegration process can be enhanced by an acceptable forum for greater truth telling.[31] He does recognize the potential drawbacks as well, noting that truth commissions are not necessarily designed for uncovering "truth," and that for some the open expression of anger can worsen social relations rather than improve them.[32] It is also possible to politicize the process. In the aftermath of the East Timor separation, Indonesia established a Peace and Stability Council (a council the government controlled). This made it politically difficult for the United Nations to set up an independent peace commission.[33]

These commissions have had various levels of success, and the most prominent tension in their use is arguably the balance between forgiveness and punishment. In the Indonesia-Timor case, the Peace Council lacked any credibility with the Timor population, but beyond the legitimacy of the organization, the Timor people contested the idea of reconciliation, at least regarding the general practice (used prominently in South Africa) of providing amnesties as part of the reconciliation. The Timorese want "reconciliation with justice." This tension presents itself in several ways. What is the relationship between the Truth Commission and the court system? In the case of transnational conflicts or crimes against humanity, how does the commission relate to international tribunals? Over what level of "crime" should these commissions have jurisdiction? What connection is there between the commission and the formal legal system (nationally and internationally)? Is the "testimony" given at the commission admissible in a formal trial? Should Truth Commissions have the power to "forgive" and absolve perpetrators of atrocities rather than seeing them punished in a court of law? Each case is unique, so planners should give great care to encouraging and assisting in reconciliation programs.

As part of the larger reconciliation project, truth-telling

and other ceremonies must have an eye toward both political and cultural acceptability. Shortcomings on either dimension diminish the value of the process, and attempts to "assist" by providing resources (particularly money) can distort the process. Most cultures have traditional practices that contribute to confessions of wrongdoing and asking for community forgiveness. These practices have the benefit of being public announcements, and implicit in these announcements is the desire of the individual to address wrongdoing and to be re-accepted into the larger society. Thus, they fall into the category of restorative (rather than retributive) justice. In almost every case, the nature of the process is relational – the former combatant admits to wrongdoing and a desire to be brought back into society, and the community allows the combatant to return. Note that this means the community *writ large* has forgiven the combatant, but not necessarily that all members of the community have done so. Nor does it mean that the abuses committed have been forgotten, only (ceremonially) forgiven. In rural Mozambique and Uganda, there were community cleansing rituals to bring people back into the community.[34] In Sierra Leone, former child combatants were taken to their former towns where they asked forgiveness from both the living and the dead. The former combatant was then stripped of the clothes symbolic of his/her past life and those clothes would be burned.[35]

In Rwanda, the system of community justice and forgiveness (known as *gacaca*) has been an attempt both to fill in for an overloaded formal justice system, but also (and more importantly) to give members a community a voice in dealing with perpetrators of the genocide.[36] There is some debate over its effectiveness, but there were few other options available for Rwanda. Certainly, attempts at reconciliation ceremonies that have cultural resonance should not be dismissed out of hand for any society struggling with post-conflict tensions. Indeed, they may provide familiar and comforting elements for a community on the road towards healing.

Reconciliation and Justice in Rwanda: The Practice of Gacaca

Rwanda experienced one of the most horrifying conflicts in the late twentieth century, including practices that made the description of "genocide" to be appropriate. The size and scale of the conflict means that there is no way all cases could be addressed through the formal court system. Recognizing both the court system's lack of capacity and the need of the larger population to gain some kind of redress, alternative methods of dispensing justice were opened. Some of these drew from prior traditions of dispute resolution, such as *gacaca*, implemented in Rwanda in 2001. "*Gacaca*" means "lawn," and represents the idea that all parties sit on the ground to talk, thereby leveling the ground between them. The hearings were publicly held, with plaintiffs, defendants, and witnesses all brought together. While the emphasis is on developing reconciliation between the parties, the judges of the *gacaca* courts can hand out significant punishments for crimes committed, including imprisonment.

Gacaca is not meant to address all cases; indeed, the most prominent cases of atrocities and genocide (especially accusations of having planned said activities) cannot be addressed by this process, but rather must be left to the formal court system. (Crimes of rape are also not addressed via *gacaca*.) The system was to be closed in June 2009, but was extended through the end of the year. Trials were continuing through early 2010. There have also been concerns that some witnesses have been traumatized by having to give testimony, and some reports of threats being made after testifying. There are other concerns involving the potential corruption of the process (either by people using the system for revenge or for political gain), as well as arguments that the court's ability to implement punishments including imprisonment meant it was less concerned with reconciliation and focused on punishment. Some critics view the process as a failed experiment. There is some truth to these criticisms, however, it is also clear that in 2001, something had to be done to deal with the overwhelming number of cases. For all of the other criticisms, *gacaca* did provide an efficient and culturally appropriate method for potential reconciliation and societal reintegration.

Further Reading: Phil Clark, *The Gacaca Courts, Post-Genocide Justice and Reconciliation in Rwanda: Justice without Lawyers* (Cambridge: Cambridge University Press, 2010).

Rigby notes that reconciliation is a process, an attempt at reframing the past and opening the way towards forgiveness. This process focuses on building trust and eventually forgiveness on the individual level, but also requires manifestations of change at higher communal/institutional levels, usually represented by some form of restitution.[37] The power of traditional methods of forgiveness and reconciliation can be aided by outside assistance, but significant caution must be exercised in this matter. While traditional ceremonies do include the presentation of objects of value, the objects themselves are not what should matter, but the notion that a process of reconciliation (restoring a peaceful relationship) is occurring. During the conflict in the Solomon Islands that led to its government's ouster in 2000 and the Australian-led intervention in 2003, government funds were used as part of "compensation" packages to traditional leaders whose group had suffered casualties. Since many of the leaders were also government officials, the process essentially became an embezzlement scheme. Rather than being part of a traditional exchange of objects (in the Solomon Islands, this includes shell money, but also things like pigs and fruit), the use of cash distorted the idea of compensation. The use of cash was not the heart of the problem, but helped exacerbate this evolving distortion in traditional practices. An earlier distortion was compensation demands being sent to provinces rather than kin groups. The government legitimized this practice in 1989 and 1996 by responding to the compensation claims.[38] (The fact that the government was the largest source of funds in the country played no small part in the motivation for targeting the government rather than sub-state groups for compensation. The government choosing to insert itself into this traditional practice perpetuated this distortion.) Finally, compensation practices are connected to restoring status by acknowledging wrongdoing. The restoration of status and the healing of relationships is the focus of these traditional ceremonies and payments, not profiteering. In Northern Malaita of the Solomons, traditional compensation actually entails the exchange of *equal* value between parties.[39] More critically, the amount of compensation was usually negotiated between parties, but by the late 1990s, compensation by demand had taken precedence.[40] This undermined any psychological value that the compensation process achieved, and also removed critical resources from the state, crippling its physical ability to institute potential reforms.

The Power of Symbols and Reconciliation

Reconciliation and practices of forgiveness must have cultural resonance, but in many cases, "culture" is itself the battleground. Ethnic, religious, or other cultural identifiers (and separators) can make the symbols themselves part of the conflict. Ironically, while scholars today are generally cognizant of the power of symbols to fuel conflict, there is little thought given to using (or rejecting) symbols in the move towards reconciliation, and in any case the questions over symbols are not considered as difficult as others (like land reform or political representation). This downplays the seriousness and difficulty of the issue. MacGinty argues that "disputes concerning symbols are often more difficult to resolve than material ones. Indeed, the 'businessman argument' approach favoured in many peace initiatives is simply unable to come to terms with the sentiment and emotion that fuels claims over symbols."[41] This problem may be an opportunity to begin a new dialogue within the community and create shared symbols. Such endeavors have to overcome a great deal of cultural and emotional inertia, but can also generate great excitement from a community that considers themselves on the cusp of making history. By definition, "new" symbols are always artificial in the beginning, but every symbol was new at some point in time. These "new" symbols require time to generate appreciation and loyalty, but there is no mistaking their power when they take hold.[42] MacGinty notes regarding a proposed memorial in Northern Ireland for *all* who have died in the conflict will not provide the cleansing sentiment that is intended unless the symbols encourage and reinforce emotions of reconciliation and forgiveness.[43]

Reintegration First?

One of the most interesting challenges to the "standard" understanding of DDR as a linear process is the implementation of the reintegration phase first. This is a difficult choice for outside agencies to consider as it entails a significant amount of risk. Initiating political reforms and a process of national and communal reconciliation in a situation where nothing has been done to address the presence of weapons can set the stage for a major resurgence of violence. As noted in the disarmament phase, regardless of its effectiveness in lowering the threat of violence, disarmament projects are very popular because of their visibility. Incidents of armed violence after disarmament do still occur, but the "public relations" disaster of an act of violence where disarmament has been downplayed or even ignored would be difficult for most international agents to overcome. Özerdem provocatively advocated this possibility for Afghanistan in 2002, noting contextual factors that would encourage the implementation of reintegration projects in the absence of significant disarmament or a major demobilization program. Özerdem points out that the cultural acceptability of weapons in the Afghan context makes comprehensive disarmament unrealistic and also that many fighters had either returned to or never left their communities, making "demobilization" a less necessary phase.[44] These points are intriguing, but the international community was quite hesitant (certainly this was understandable at the political level) to deviate from "standard" practices. Indeed, the "reintegration first" idea was actually implemented in Tajikistan, and while there has been very little violence since the end of the conflict, the experience suggests the limits to prioritizing reintegration in this fashion.

Reintegration First? The Case of Tajikistan

Tajikistan offers one of the most interesting cases of a DDR experience that not only drew little international assistance, but focused first and foremost on the reintegration process. To be sure, there were several factors that allowed Tajikistan to reintegrate first that are unlikely to occur in other situations, but the case does highlight starkly the point that the DDR process need not be lockstep. The experience also suggests that prioritizing reintegration and overlooking issues like inadequate disarmament rates can build significant trust among the parties and curtail a great number of potential spoilers to the process. As a cautionary note, the Tajikistan experience also shows some of the consequences in not emphasizing some aspects of disarmament and demobilization earlier in the process.

After the breakup of the Soviet Union, Tajikistan found itself caught up in a civil war from 1992 to 1997. Some elements fought for increasing democratization (including groups calling for a greater role for Islam in the governing of the society), while others fought for some continuation of the status quo style of government. The former elements coalesced into the United Tajik Opposition (UTO), receiving some support from Tajik elements in Afghanistan, while the pro-government forces were supported by Uzbekistan (and later by Russia) due to fears of spreading Militant Islam. These concerns reached their height in 1996 with the fall of Kabul to the Taliban. The shift in the historical context allowed newly-appointed Russian Foreign Minister Evgeny Primakov to negotiate a compromise and end the fighting.

Social reintegration was the priority and the Tajik government was willing to risk incomplete disarmament and demobilization to achieve it. Rather than focus on disarming the opposing armed groups, the Tajik government ignored evidence of inadequate weapons surrender. Furthermore, in the reconstitution of the national security force, entire units of the UTO were incorporated, essentially preserving their command structures in an effort to maintain trust and reduce uncertainty for individual combatants.

Further Reading: Stina Torjesen and S. Neil MacFarlane, "R before D: the case of post-conflict reintegration in Tajikistan," *Conflict, Security and Development* 7, 2 (June 2007).

What Next? After Reintegration

No matter where it is "phased" in terms of implementation, truly successful DDR implementation is measured by how well "reintegrated" are the former combatants and the communities they are now living in. Reintegration may be the "end" of the DDR project, but it is only the beginning in the journey to establish a long-term peace. Now, the community is even more likely to have to deal with problems without the attention (or assistance) of the international community that has moved on to another issue. Regardless of the terminology, a community that has gone through a "complete" DDR process has more accurately had former combatants "reinserted" into their communities, with "reintegration" an ongoing and constant journey. It is in this "post-DDR" phase that the commitment of the people (both the combatants and the community) and the domestic government (and in some cases, regional governments) is at its most critical. The DDR project opens political and social "breathing space," but the encouraging of a long-term peace extends far beyond its abilities.

CHAPTER SIX

Challenges and Conclusions

The "So What?" Question: Does DDR "Work"?

In a 2009 edited volume on post-conflict stabilization and reconstruction, Robert Muggah questioned the framework and application of DDR programs, arguing that they have not lived up to their promise. Simply put, there was little evidence that DDR programs had contributed to the establishment of peace.[1] If Muggah's point is accurate, then three possibilities arise (though they are not necessarily mutually exclusive). First, the DDR project is a chimera, offering nothing more than sound and fury and the illusion of achievement. (This is a criticism that frequently arises in the disarmament stage). This conclusion is often drawn when it seems the DDR project is simply being repeated over and over again. (Colombia is a clear example of this. Since the 1970s, there have been nine separate DDR processes with different groups).[2] If this is the case, DDR may satisfy a sense of altruism by outside powers, but does little or nothing to alleviate the underlying issues of the conflict. A second possibility is the DDR project is consistently oversold, thereby giving a variety of audiences an expectation that it will accomplish far more than is reasonable in its implementation. There may be a variety of political reasons to suggest a greater impact on the part of the DDR project than is realistic, but continuing to do so only disappoints both the affected community and domestic supporters as time goes on. The final possibility regarding the lack of evidence of a connection between DDR and peace is that researchers and practitioners have not been looking at the right things, or at least not considering them the right way. While there is much to be cynical about regarding the application of DDR and the resulting "peace" that emerges from the process, there are enough points of success to suggest the latter two conclusions to be the more likely cases. Short-term political demands can lead to a tendency to exaggerate the potential impacts of DDR. On the issue of assessment, a continuing theme throughout the cases examined is the great power and importance of perception (especially of the affected community) of progress. Perception and its power is very difficult to quantify, and can lead to its impacts being downplayed in analysis and official reports.

The most difficult challenge faced by those implementing any DDR project may be the disconnect between expectations (of both the affected community and the agencies/ governments implementing DDR) and reality. Beyond political exaggeration, much of this difference can be attributed to terminology and the expectations that the terminology creates. In particular, where does "reintegration" end? Is there such a thing as "complete" reintegration into a society? DDR practitioners are still trying to come to grips with the issue of "incomplete" disarmament, and this phenomenon has been recognized and discussed for at least a decade. Shortening the timeframe of DDR (by considering "reinsertion" rather than "reintegration") may be one way of managing these expectations for combatants.

There are official understandings and definitions of the time and scale of the DDR project, but putting them on paper and actually implementing them in the field are very different things. Even beyond the issue of implementation, the *perception* of the affected community that DDR is "complete" is not tied to any official timetable. The setting of "end dates" is easy

enough, the achievement (or even the fostering) of beneficial "end states" is significantly more difficult. However, the
latter is the only meaningful goal for any post-conflict stabilization program. Themnér suggests an interesting challenge
that he refers to as the "catch-22" of reintegration assistance.
Themnér poses the question: if reintegration packages do not
actually generate income opportunities, then why do most
combatants not return to the use of violence? He suggests
two possibilities. First, reintegration assistance simply buys
time, allowing for what is essentially a "cooling off" period
for the combatants. Second, there may be a developing sense
that combatants have a "right" to such assistance. Therefore,
governments and international agencies have to have these
programs, even they do not "work." Otherwise, combatants
may feel cheated out of their "deserved" assistance and in fact
return to violence.[3]

Muggah's evaluation of the DDR project is not all negative. Most interestingly, he notes that although a 2004 survey
revealed no statistically significant correlations between DDR
and peace, it did indicate an increase in the *perception* of security after the implementation of DDR.[4] This is an extremely
important insight, as it suggests a need for more subjective
measures of performance. Indeed, Muggah advocates the
greater use of evaluation criteria drawn from the affected communities themselves. The participation of these communities
"allows for a bottom-up articulation of benchmarks that are
more closely aligned to local interests and expectations."[5]
Doing so enhances the connection between the international
agencies and the affected communities' perception of the *purpose and effectiveness* of the DDR project.

In nearly every case of DDR implementation, two important tensions remain unresolved. One is a tension at the
operational level. Is the DDR project best implemented as an
integrated, holistic project, or does focusing on the distinct

phases of DDR allow for more effective implementation? This operational tension is really a manifestation of a deeper, strategic question for policymakers considering a DDR project. Simply put, what is DDR intended to achieve? Should DDR focus on the short-to-medium term provision of security (defined as the absence of destabilizing violence) or should the role of DDR take into consideration longer-term issues such as economic and social development? When does "DDR" end, and the adjective of "post-conflict" become a less meaningful description for a society?

Security vs. Development

The "security vs. development" debate in DDR is a chronic one in the literature. Ebbinghaus on Sierra Leone, for example, argues that a stronger emphasis on security would actually benefit DDR and prospects for long-term peace. A focus on security issues allows the military/peacekeeping force to deal with areas they are more comfortable with and not end up making potentially unrealistic commitments.[6] Contrarily, Verwimp and Verpoorten suggest regarding Rwanda that the government and international community focused too narrowly on security. By doing so, DDR agencies missed that concerns over economic development and future livelihood were more important (at least, in Rwanda) for encouraging participation in DDR.[7]

Every DDR experience will exhibit "lessons learned" that point to a focus either on security or development. There is no question that both factors are necessary (if not sufficient) to achieve long-term peace, but a definite answer as to which one to prioritize is impossible. The specific context of the situation at hand will dictate whether a focus on security or a larger focus on development is more effective. This uncertainty is what makes attempts at a universal theory of DDR so maddening, but embracing such ambiguity is not often the hallmark of international agencies. (In fairness, national governments hardly do any better with such uncertainty).

On some level, this question is not really about security vs. development. The provision of security is in fact intended to provide opportunities for greater development. The real question is one of time and perception. Can those implementing the DDR program accept security risks in the short term in an effort to build trust in the community, thereby creating greater operating space and the potential for long-term development? The more specific question is then, what *type* of short-term risks in security build trust as opposed to increase perceptions of fear and insecurity? A preoccupation with security is especially problematic for third-party agents intervening in an area and following on with the DDR project. It is greatly tempting for outside parties to emphasize the security aspect because of political sensitivities for the populations "back home" due to fear of casualties. (This can really distort the situation when the overarching concern becomes the safety of the foreign nationals rather than fulfilling the mission of stabilizing the post-conflict community). Attempting to create a "completely secure" environment simply encourages spoilers to bide their time. It can also hinder the creation of trust due to the perception from the affected community that their security is only being maintained through force.

Integration or Phasing?

There seems little question that a truly successful DDR program integrates all of its aspects towards a single goal, but what does that mean in implementation? Muggah notes the basic assumption that the three aspects of DDR are mutually reinforcing,[8] but implementation suggests that a lack of communication or a disagreement over the focus of the

DDR project can mean the phases do not contribute towards a common goal. Civic and Miklaucic say it best, "By anointing a complex set of relationships with an acronym . . . we endow it with a misleadingly singular character, and significant tensions within the component elements are obscured."[9] Practitioners do need to recognize that the ultimate goal of DDR is to move a post-conflict society towards greater peace and security, but recognizing where compromises can be made in each particular phase of the process is extremely difficult. When does forcing a greater proportion of the society to disarm enhance the security situation? When does this contribute to greater insecurity and make the situation more precarious? The answer to these questions is greatly dependent on the situation, and the point is to give the question serious consideration rather than assume any universal equation between disarmament and peace. DDR can be implemented in phases or in an integrated fashion, but regardless of its implementation, the program must be "mentally" integrated by those implementing the program as well as reinforcing positive perceptions of safety within the affected community. It is the ends that are central, not the means. If practitioners keep the overall goal of increasing peace and security in mind, then the "acceptable levels of failure" in any specific phase of the program become easier to develop and negotiate. Indeed, this insight leads to the somewhat provocative idea that in some cases, not all "phases" of DDR should be implemented. This is not just because they are not necessary, but because they may in fact be counterproductive.

Furthermore, while the value of integrating the phases in DDR is being recognized, the personnel actually implementing the particular phases are usually not the same people or (more critically) not from the same organization. Since there is often a "handover" from military organizations to civilian ones in the transition from disarmament to demobilization, an understanding of shared goals and mutually reinforcing programs is critical. This requires greater communication between military and civilian organizations, both between and within governments as well as international organizations and military coalitions. Unlike Botticelli's Venus, the communication behind an effective interagency relationship for DDR will not instantly spring, fully formed. The communication and trust is part of a longer relationship, especially within a government. For most cases, this will most likely be a government assisting with DDR in another country. The United States has attempted to address some of the shortcomings in its interagency processes and relationships.[10] These relationships will take time to bear fruit, but they must start now rather than wait for the next situation. For nations and agencies working together today in Iraq and Afghanistan (not to mention ongoing DDR programs in several other countries), the struggle to develop and maintain not "best practices," but "good relationships"' should be the goal.

Even a highly integrated DDR program is only the first step toward establishing peace. Issues of forgiveness, reconciliation, and even technical issues (like the longer-term management of small arms and light weapons) require capabilities and timetables that extend far beyond even the most integrated DDR program.[11] This means that greater coordination at the planning stages is of even greater importance. It also requires a level of understanding of the ultimate goals of DDR and the ability to assume certain levels of risk on the part of the leadership, both on the ground and in government.

Leadership Issues

Every DDR project faces several levels of leadership challenges. First, any DDR program with international involvement has to deal with the "international vs. domestic" leadership problem.

In Afghanistan, Japan took on the lead international role for DDR. Japan has been very eager to find a greater niche in international involvement over the last decade, and has been especially interested in being involved in assisting projects that encourage international peace. Japan certainly brought significant technical expertise to the disarmament and demobilization of forces in Afghanistan, but had to be extremely careful with many aspects of its involvement. The anti-war clause of Japan's constitution has usually been interpreted by its government as barring the use of military personnel abroad. This meant that some of Japan's DDR actions in Afghanistan caused significant controversy in Japan.[12] None of the actions would have been as politically problematic for any other country.[13] In other cases, past colonial relationships can make DDR assistance more politically problematic, especially within the affected communities. In such instances, it is easy for spoilers and cynics to question the motivation of former colonial masters to intervene. Finally, the motivations of regional powers can also be brought into question. Is the intervention an attempt to establish greater influence, even hegemony, over a region? There is some inclination by the United Nations for regionally led interventions from the 1990s onward. Using regional organizations and powers to lead these operations has the advantage of using a state with a fair amount of both resources and cultural knowledge of the affected area. The disadvantage is that their motives can be put into question.[14]

More obvious leadership challenges will usually reside within the domestic government and the local communities. Since the legitimacy of the government is already questionable due to the experience of armed conflict, a great deal depends on its aptitude in handling its role in the post-conflict environment. Militias develop to address security threats the state has proven unable (an issue of state competence) or unwilling (an issue of state capability) to address. The post-conflict state has to address these twin dimensions of competence and capability, but has to do so in different ways. Many issues of state competence can be addressed by technical fixes – increases in personnel, supply, or training. Perceived issues of state capability, however, touch at a different form of insecurity – the perception that the state–citizen relationship is damaged (or nonexistent) and the state is not concerned with their well-being. The latter problem is a great deal more insidious, as an increase in capabilities does not mean an increase in security. Indeed, if the government is the source of threat, then greater capability equates to a greater threat. Outside governments and agencies should also consider this point carefully, as the technical fixes are generally those that outside agencies can assist with in the short term. While outside agencies can assist with issues of governance and rule of law, in the end the effectiveness of those programs can only be found in the perception and trust of the citizens to their community, and the community to its government.

Community Focus vs. Targeting Individuals

A perpetual problem for DDR implementation is the perception that combatants are being "rewarded" for their past actions. Even in cases where the combatants are part of the "winning" side, the issue of what resources former combatants may now receive (in contrast to the general population) can often cause significant resentment. Reintegration and reconstruction in the aftermath of a violent conflict encompasses the individual, community and national levels. The relationship between the reintegration of the combatants and the reconstruction of the community is a symbiotic one; one will not be successful without the other. Handling this relationship is a delicate balancing act, as an overemphasis on one side or the other can exacerbate tensions and divisions rather than relieve them.

"Special" consideration of combatants to some extent is unavoidable. Combatants are the most likely spoilers in the initial post-conflict context. Their ability to reignite the conflict is the most significant threat in the opening stages of the DDR/peacebuilding process. Therefore, incentives that lower the potential for their return to violence have to be included in the planning and handling of the post-conflict situation. Doing so early in the DDR program ameliorates the immediate threat of resurgent violence. Continuing to do so as the process continues, however, increases the perception that combatants are being rewarded for their combatant status and this exacerbates the psychological divide that DDR (and longer-term programs) is ostensibly intended to overcome (namely, the civilian–combatant divide). Targeting DDR assistance to the entire community too early in the process, however, does not address the potential of spoilers. If communities are provided with assistance to rebuild with no incentive to reinsert combatants, then there is less motivation for any community to accept these individuals.

Jennings offers one potential approach to balancing the combatant–community divide here. She argues that stressing security over development goals (essentially de-linking disarmament and demobilization from reintegration) is more effective in situations where clear distinctions between "civilians" and "combatants" can be made. This means that providing early assistance to former combatants early on is politically and socially acceptable if these divisions are clear. If the context is such that the past experiences (in terms of trauma) and future outlook (in terms of economic development) between those who participated in the conflict and those "merely" affected by it are much closer together, then the emphasis should be on larger development goals.[15] Kingma reinforces this point, suggesting that as time goes on (and the distinctions between civilians and combatants become more blurred), reintegration assistance should be more widely distributed among the community rather than targeted towards individual combatants.[16] Continuing to provide "special" assistance to reinserted individuals over time maintains the distinction that must be overcome – the idea that the former combatant is set apart from the rest of the community.

DDR: Destination or Journey?

In the final analysis, the above debates are less important for the answers derived (since these conclusions will always be contested), but rather for the discussions themselves. For any large organization, there is an overwhelming temptation to template successful practices from one case to another without reflection. Organizations and practitioners try to mechanize success. The motivations to do so are understandable, but the contexts for each post-conflict event are too idiosyncratic to force any template (beyond the most overarching) upon it. Success is not found in the practice/tactic in and of itself, but in a deeper understanding of its underlying rationale. The point is not the success of the tactic, but an understanding of why it succeeded that is important for future practitioners. The practice is not the point, but its underlying logic must be understood. No program will ever go perfectly, and while some setbacks may be insurmountable, others can be overcome. Recognizing this difference enhances significantly the ability to create contextually appropriate measures of success. More importantly, this leads to a greater understanding of how much "breathing space" a DDR project has in which to operate. In other words, certain types and levels of failure may in fact be "acceptable."

"Acceptable" Levels of Failure

More than any quantitative measure, DDR is about the *perceptions* of the community that it is safer. Security, like the creation of nationalism and community, is "imagined" to a great extent. This does not mean the community can be lied to about the objective issues such as the number of violent incidents or the competence of the security force meant to protect them, but the critical value is how the threats (and their sources) are *perceived* by the community, not the threats themselves. No negotiation will ever be perfect, and planning for and dealing with potential spoilers to the process is better than denying the possibility of their rise. During talks either for an initial peace agreement or under the terms and conditions of those agreements, disgruntled fighters can attempt to block the talks with an upsurge of violence. These spoilers can cripple any advances. However, it is not simply the level of violence that gives the spoiler their power. Indeed, in some cases an increasing level of violence is an indication of the increasing marginalization of these individuals who are now pushing for greater acts of violence in an effort to remain relevant. The power of the spoiler is not inherent in the capability to perpetrate acts of violence; it is in fact not inherent in the spoiler at all. The spoiler's power derives from the *reactions* (both physical and perceptual) of the other groups to these acts of violence. A group committing acts of violence in opposition to peace negotiations can make those negotiations moot only if the acts and the negotiations are connected in the perceptions of the negotiating groups and the larger population. If these acts are instead seen as a rise in nonpolitical criminal violence, then they will have less impact on the negotiations themselves.

All governments fail at some point and to some extent. The issue is whether the population will "accept" this failure as an understandable reality rather than a commentary on the state's legitimacy. Crime is the most obvious example for this phenomenon. No government can completely eliminate acts of violence or other forms of criminality. The "failure" to eliminate all violence from a society, however, does not diminish the perceived authority of the state unless other conditions are met. Is a specific, identifiable group being "targeted" for violence/criminality because of their group identity (ethnicity, religious affiliation, other forms of status)? This condition is probably necessary, but is not sufficient in and of itself. Targeting the rich, for example, for crimes of robbery does not immediately draw into question the viability of the state. The issue of targeting must be connected to the level or lack of response. A government whose security forces are *unable* to address large levels of criminal violence may still be part of a legitimate (albeit a weak) state, while a security force *unwilling* to do so undermines the credibility of the state as an impartial actor. The issue here is not necessarily the failure of the security force to protect, but the reasons (or perceived reasons) behind the failure.

The rhetoric of the perpetrators and how the larger public views them also contributes to the "acceptability" of failure. Groups fighting ostensibly for a political cause are trying to subvert a state's authority in the eyes of the larger public. Acts of violence perpetrated by these groups suggest the state as illegitimate (the central grievance) and/or ineffective (the inability to defeat the insurgent group). In this case, acts of violence undermine the state and contribute to the perception that it is losing. However, states confronting organized crime may see high levels of violence, but while the public may criticize a government's failures in defeating a criminal organization, most criminal organizations do not pose a *political* threat to the state. It is therefore not the acts of violence themselves that undermine the state, but their purpose and justifications, and how powerfully those justifications resonate with the larger populace, that give the violence "meaning." The ongoing development of criminal gangs in Colombia, with membership drawn from both guerrilla groups and self-defense forces mentioned previously is one example of this evolution. El Salvador's current gang violence is certainly problematic, but gangs such as *Mara Salvatrucha* (also known as MS-13) may offer a diminished *political* threat to the Salvadoran government since their identity and organization lack the ideological/political legitimacy of an insurgent group.[17] The Abu Sayyaf Group (ASG) in the southern Philippines also exhibits this phenomenon. Founded by members who had fought against the Soveits in Afghanistan, the ASG sought the establishment of a "caliphate" in the mostly Muslim areas of the southern Philippines. When its founder and leader was killed by Philippine security forces in 1998, it devolved into a kidnapping-for-profit organization. This "transformation" greatly diminished its political legitimacy (Al Qaeda disassociated itself from the ASG at this time)[18] and allowed the government to make significant political inroads against the group. In some cases, then, rising criminality suggests some success in quelling more politically oriented violence. This may prove cold comfort for those still under threat, but it can in fact be an indicator that government reforms are having a positive effect in addressing some of the political grievances that help fuel the insurgent movement.

The Problem is Not Identifying the Problem

As the previous chapters show, the problems confronting the integration of the phases of DDR and the successful demobilization of irregular forces are not hard to identify, but very hard to solve. Scholars have noted the political dimensions of the DDR project, pointing out the biasing of the more technical aspects of the endeavor, and the shortcomings that arise from that. However, this recognition has not really manifested as reforms at the operational level.[19] Perhaps even more important than the political factors, the more psychological aspects are also being recognized at the strategic level, but have yet to be implemented operationally in a systemic manner. Again, the problem is easy to identify, but how to address these issues is usually specific to each case. Usually, the amount of time, resources, expertise, and/or political commitment, especially from the international community, is almost always "not enough."

Regardless of the idiosyncrasies of each DDR experience, the international community must assist war-ravaged communities in their recovery. In most cases, the country or area will not have the economic or technical resources to handle DDR alone. However, *supporting* the effort with technical expertise or financial aid cannot then devolve into the international community *directing* the program. Berdal cogently identifies the appropriate role of outside actors in the DDR process, noting that "external actors cannot replace political commitment nor can they generate political momentum in the absence of trust and will among the parties. They can, however, by the manner in which support is extended, discourage defection from a peace process, thus strengthening, however subtly, the degree of commitment that does exist."[20]

The technical expertise and other resources that outside parties bring to the DDR project are only part of the equation. Third parties bring to the post-conflict situation their own political interests as well as any historical and institutional baggage that may be associated with the context of the conflict. "Outside" nations with a particular interest in a country or region frequently have a checkered historical relationship with the region (usually a prior colonial relationship). Despite their greater resources and some cultural understanding then, these third parties are often less legitimate as "impartial agents" to many in the domestic community.

Disarmament

It is not the number of weapons collected that is important. In fact, disarmament does not really have to be about the weapons at all, but about recognizing and modifying a situation where the use of violence to settle disputes is accepted, even preferred, to the mechanisms of the state. On the other hand, the visible and verifiable collection and destruction of weapons can contribute to the development of that trust.[21] Both perspectives are correct. The success of the disarmament phase lies in its contribution to the creation and/or building of trust between the parties. Disarmament is not always the place where peacebuilding starts, sometimes (perhaps most times) it actually symbolizes the trust already developed. DDR in some cases should be reconceptualized as "d"DR, situating disarmament more clearly as a subset of demobilization. Whether it occurs "first" or not, some level of disarmament should probably happen fairly early in the DDR process, and if there is a time that the international community will pay attention to the problem, it will be in these early stages. The technical expertise of many organizations to handle disarmament (indeed, many are very good because of almost constantly working somewhere) should be leveraged, but weapons collection will not be the most significant achievement towards building a lasting peace.

While it is understandable that disarmament gets the attention it does, this preoccupation has to be overcome. Disarmament can be a very visible event, but visibility is not necessarily progress. A focus on technical issue of weapons collection ignores greater cultural understandings of the roles weapons play within specific societies. Weapons can and do have symbolic power in many societies, but *this does not mean their possession creates actual insecurity.* Understanding and taking advantage of this subtle nuance could be highly beneficial in avoiding the continuing overemphasis on weapons collection over the creation and encouragement of an atmosphere of trust. In a community emerging from conflict, growing relationships of trust can make the presence of weapons less "dangerous" just as often (if not more often) as the reduction of the number of weapons in a community opens the way for trust to develop. The relationship is symbiotic, but not unidirectional.

Demobilization

Understanding demobilization primarily as a psychological experience rather than a physicial one is arguably the most important insight. There are certainly physical manifestations of demobilization (removal of uniforms and rank insignia, the distancing of individuals from former commanders), and the psychological separation can be aided by physical distance, but it is the mental shift that is critical. The ability to separate parties effectively as they demobilize can even partially substitute for disarmament, since this separation of hostile parties can make weapons possession less important. However, physical distance can enhance psychological divisions and make societal reintegration that much harder. Geographic separation can lead to voluntary segregation and division. This division has its benefits in the early stages of disarmament and demobilization, but may reinforce psychological or political divisions and feelings of difference. These perceptions will make reintegration much more difficult.

Reintegration

Reintegration is the most political of all the phases in DDR, so developing and maintaining enough political will (both in the affected community and for domestic communities of the outside governments) to sustain the program through the inevitable setbacks in implementation is absolutely critical. The propagation of "Rs" (reinsertion, repatriation, reconciliation, just to name a few) in the literature suggest the reintegration phase of the DDR project continues to be the most elusive in terms of understanding, much less success. In the end, it is likely the only phase that matters. Where "reintegration" actually ends is an impossible question to answer, and many scholars and agencies are stressing "reinsertion" rather than "reintegration" as a description for their actions.[22] This is more than semantics. The former term may carry fewer long-term expectations with it (for both the domestic and international communities), and managing expectations and perceptions at this stage is critical to the overall success of the DDR project. The reintegration of combatants into the post-conflict society, and the development of a society where both the term "post-conflict" and "ex-combatant" are no longer meaningful labels, is likely to require a longer time-span than the international community has the interest, or the legitimacy, to oversee. This means that while international assistance will undoubtedly be required, it is imperative that governments, regional organizations, and local community efforts take the lead (and most importantly, prioritize funding for these projects) as international attention will inevitably fade over time.

As the distinction between "combatant" and "civilian" becomes less meaningful within the community, financial and other assistance should be disbursed towards the larger community rather than to individual combatants. In post-conflict situations where this distance is not great in the first place, reintegration assistance that targets individual combatants can cause resentment, and even in situations where special incentives for combatants is a good idea, over time doing so will perpetuate the distinction that the assistance is meant to eliminate.

For longer term projects, true "reintegration" of a society will no doubt require the development and fostering of culturally appropriate and powerful symbols and methods of reconciliation. This may or may not include structures such as truth commissions, but if they do, their proper role must be assessed and agreed upon before they are implemented. Any international assistance, especially those that attempt to incentivize cultural forgiveness processes with modern material benefits, should be attempted only with great caution, if at all.

Planning and Evaluation

It is clear that theory recognizes the need to consider DDR as an integrated rather than a sequential program, but how that understanding is manifested in practice is still difficult to articulate. Establishing national government "ownership" of a DDR program is sensible if there is a reasonable expectation that this will help more than it will hinder progress. Some level of national buy-in is necessary, but attempting to give the national government too much authority in the process can be problematic both operationally and politically. The idea of interagency and international communication has to go further than recognizing a basic modicum of security is needed to implement other programs, but this recognition is certainly a good start. The necessity of a baseline of security for establishing any complementary project (whether by non-government organizations or non-military government agencies) is critical. Nothing can be built in an atmosphere of a high potential for violence, but mitigating this potential only through force (rather than by building and encouraging trust) only creates a situation where underlying tensions build and will explode when the superior military force is no longer present.

Planners should also recognize the issues of international contributions as well. Countries with the political willingness to lead a DDR program may have the technical expertise to do so, but may have their motives questioned by groups in the post-conflict state. This is a continual dilemma for states acting within a former colony, or more generally for the United States as the world's sole superpower. (Arguably, this dilemma arises long before the DDR stage. More likely, the debate over motivations occur while the very idea of intervention – especially those led by the military – is under discussion). Berdal notes in general that the best roles for third-party military forces in DDR fall into three major categories: verification/monitoring, logistic support, and demining.[23] While these activities are generally technical in nature, their real benefit is the psychological impact the practices can have on all concerned parties. Demining is overall a technical project and can be a powerful confidence-building measure for all parties. (Truly comprehensive demining programs also open up significant stretches of land that may be used as resources for bargaining with recalcitrant individuals or groups). The third-party force almost invariably has greater resources than national powers, and so the ability to provide logistic support both eases the use of domestic resources and in some cases can be an implicit "show of force" that can help dissuade potential spoilers. The ability of the third party to be an honest broker in verifying disarmament and demobilization contributes to the increase in trust in the post-conflict situation.

The last problem is one of assessment. Identifying "combatants" early on and considering what criteria to use to measure their demobilization and reinsertion is critical. As time goes on and the emotional divide between civilians and combatants grows smaller, the implementation of more community-oriented reintegration and development programs can follow. A greater amount of resources may allow for the instituting of more community-based programs to alleviate any resentment toward former combatants, but choices still have to be made. With finite resources, should agencies focus on the biggest potential spoilers or on the group/community that can make the biggest positive impact? Because the real impact of the DDR project is so difficult to measure, agencies often fall into the trap of using "measures of effort" rather than "measures of effectiveness." While the former are generally easy to measure, the latter may not be quantifiable at all.

The issue is not really about identifying "combatants" at the later point, but rather about identifying potential spoilers. Muggah argues that development agencies recognize the different incentives for why combatants join armed groups (and why they will consider demobilization and reintegration), but security professionals often miss this point.[24] This suggests that regardless of whether DDR programs should be security-focused or more development-focused, communicating insights between the military and development professionals needs to be practiced on a regular (and regularized) basis. Personalities matter more than organizational structures, but structures can be built to encourage and nurture those individuals inclined to and adept at interagency cooperation. More importantly, the relationships and trust needed for effective interagency cooperation must be in place long before the DDR project's implementation. The cooperation needed for effective DDR, especially those that include a "handover" of responsibility from military to civilian organizations, should not be continually relearned for each particular crisis.

Final Thoughts

For successful DDR, social context and psychological shifts will *always* trump bureaucratic arrangements and technocratic processes. While it is certainly the intention of these arrangements and processes to lead to the social context and shifts for successful DDR, many of the cases noted previously show that oftentimes, the things that can be *measured* are not the things that *matter*. The DDR process may have a general framework, but that framework must be extremely flexible. (Indeed, despite the perhaps incessant criticism of technocratic processes throughout this book, the point is not to dismiss these practices, but to understand the context in which they will be applied most effectively). More to the point, DDR's agents (and their superiors) must be mentally flexible in understanding the varying contexts of the situation rather than overlaying a previously successful "model." In some cases, the removal of weapons inspires trust between conflicting parties; while in others, ongoing negotiations develop trust that then lead to the willingness to disarm. In demobilization, the removal of command structures is generally the sought-after goal; but in some cases, maintaining these structures can alleviate the psychological uncertainty for many ex-combatants. What Kilcullen argues in the Afghanistan counterinsurgency context is no less true here. "The challenge for commanders and assessment staffs is . . . not to template previously useful metrics, but rather constantly develop and apply new indicators, based on a shared diagnosis of what the conflict is, and what is driving it."[25]

The project is difficult, and actual progress is more about context and perception than number of weapons or combatants. Attempts to template practices without a clear understanding of the context provide activity, but often little accomplishment. To say the problem as "all in the mind" is not a dismissal of the true difficulties in addressing the issues. Indeed, it only reinforces the point that the mind is the most powerful weapon of all, for good or ill. DDR contributes to long-term peace, but is only one of the steps toward it. DDR only provides some breathing space for actors to engage with each other, build trust, and attempt forgiveness. DDR begins this process, and should be connected with longer-term programs directed toward establishing peace, but DDR does not complete the journey towards peace. Jackson's words on Africa resonate for every DDR program: "we now understand that war is at root a social and political construction rather than an inevitable condition. The implications of this are more than just ontological: if [wars] can be constructed by ethnic entrepreneurs, despots and warlords, then they can also be deconstructed by activists, journalists, peacemakers and the *ordinary people* who suffer them."[26] DDR is the critical first step in the journey towards peace, and in the end, the struggle for peace is the only one worth fighting.

Notes

1 INTRODUCTION

1 Most prominently there was the publication in China of
Unrestricted Warfare, a work by two colonels speculating on how
one country could defeat a technologically superior opponent.
The work was subsequently translated into English and was the
cause of great discussion in many policy circles regarding China's
intentions and rise as a near-peer competitor. See Qiao Liang and
Wang Xiangsui, *Unrestricted Warfare* (Beijing: PLA Literature
and Arts Publishing House, February 1999), http://www.
missilethreat.com/repository/doclib/19990200-LiangXiangsui-
unrestrictedwar.pdf (accessed December 1, 2011).
2 Phil Williams, *Criminals, Militias, and Insurgents: Organized
Crime in Iraq* (Carlisle: Strategic Studies Institute, 2009), 50.
3 Robert Muggah, "No Magic Bullet: A Critical Perspective on
Disarmament, Demobilization and Reintegration (DDR) and
Weapons Reduction in Post-Conflict Contexts" *The Round Table*
94 (April 2005), 240.
4 Headquarters, Department of the Army, *Counterinsurgency* FM
3–24 (Washington, DC: Headquarters, Department of the Army,
2006).
5 Wray Johnson, "Doctrine for Irregular Warfare: Déjà Vu All Over
Again?" *Marine Corps University Journal* 2, 1 (Spring 2011), 37 n10.
6 Most notably, the manual acknowledges David Galula's
Counterinsurgency Warfare: Theory and Practice (1964) and Sir
Robert Thompson's *Defeating Communist Insurgency: The Lessons
of Malaya and Vietnam* (1966).
7 US Army Colonel Gian Gentile is one of the most prominent
advocates of this position. See his "Let's Build an Army to Win *All
Wars*," *Joint Forces Quarterly* 52, 1 (2009), 27–33.

8 Patrick Bishop, *Ground Truth* (London: Harper Press, 2009), 194.
9 Mats R. Berdal, *Disarmament and Demobilisation after Civil Wars*, Adelphi Paper 303 (Oxford: International Institute for Strategic Studies, 1996), 21.

2 THE HISTORY AND EVOLUTION OF DDR

1 Fred Charles Iklé, *Every War Must End*, Second Edition, Revised (New York: Columbia University Press, 2005).
2 Mark Knight, "Expanding the DDR Model: Politics and Organisations," *Journal of Security Sector Management* 6, 1 (March 2008), 3.
3 Jennifer M. Hazen, "Understanding 'Reintegration' within Postconflict Peacebuilding: Making the Case for 'Reinsertion' First and Better Linkages Thereafter," in Melanne A. Civic and Michael Miklaucic, eds, *Monopoly of Force: The Nexus of DDR and SSR* (Washington, DC: NDU Press, 2011), 111. Hazen (125, n4) further notes that the Stockholm Initiative on Disarmament, Demobilisation and Reintegration's *SIDDR Final Report 2006* says there were 36 DDR projects between 1994 and 2006.
4 United Nations Disarmament, Demobilization and Reintegration Resource Center, http://www.unddr.org/countryprogrammes. php (accessed October 29, 2011). The countries listed were Afghanistan, Burundi, Central African Republic, Cote d'Ivoire, Democratic Republic of Congo, Haiti, Liberia, Nepal, Sierra Leone, Solomon Islands, Somalia, Sudan, and Uganda.
5 Ian Douglas, Colin Gleichmann, Michael Odenwald, Kees Steenken, and Adrian Wilkinson, *Disarmament, Demobilisation, and Reintegration: A Practical Field and Classroom Guide* (Frankfurt: Druckerei Hassmüller Graphische Betriebe GmbH and Co., 2004), 17.
6 David J. Francis, "Introduction," in David J. Francis, ed., *Civil Militia: Africa's Intractable Security Menace?* (Burlington, VT: Ashgate, 2005), 2.
7 Atreyee Sen and David Pratten, "Global Vigilantes: Perspectives on Justice and Violence," in David Pratten and Atreyee Sen, eds, *Global Vigilantes* (New York: Columbia University Press, 2008), 9.

8 Chris Alden, Monika Thakur, and Matthew Arnold, *Militias and the Challenges of Post-Conflict Peace: Silencing the Guns* (London: Zed Books, 2011), 4.

9 Alden, Thakur, and Arnold, *Militias*, 4, emphasis added.

10 Francis, "Introduction," 2.

11 Keen and Marriage both point out the fine line between "soldier" and "rebel" at the individual level in Sierra Leone and the Democratic Republic of the Congo, respectively. These similarities make it easy for an individual to switch sides during the conflict, but governments and other agencies running DDR programs will still make the distinction between members of a formal military and a "rebel" group. See David Keen, *Conflict and Colllusion in Sierra Leone* (James Currey: Oxford, 2005), and Zoë Marriage, "Flip-Flop Rebel, Dollar Soldier: Demobilisation in the Democratic Republic of Congo," *Conflict, Security, and Development* 7, 2 (June 2007).

12 Véronique Dudouet, "Nonstate Armed Groups and the Politics of Postwar Security Governance," in Melanne A. Civic and Michael Miklaucic, eds, *Monopoly of Force: The Nexus of DDR and SSR* (Washington, DC: NDU Press, 2011), 19.

13 Max Manwaring argues that the purpose of gang violence is irrelevant, and that its very impact undermines the sovereignty of the state. See Max G. Manwaring, *Urban Gangs: The New Insurgency* (Carlisle Barracks: Strategic Studies Institute, 2005). Manwaring's argument is interesting, but at first glance, it seems unlikely that DDR would be implemented the same way with a criminal gang as it would with an armed group. This supposition does bear further consideration but is outside this book's scope.

14 Jared Cohen, *Children of Jihad: A Young American's Travels Among the Youth of the Middle East* (New York: Gotham Books, 2007), 145.

15 Henri Boshoff, "The Demobilisation, Disarmament, and Reintegration Process in the Democratic Republic of the Congo. A Never-ending story!" Institute for Security Studies Situation Report (2 July 2007), 6.

16 Sean McFate, "There's a New Sheriff in Town: DDR-SSR and the Monopoly of Force," in Melanne A. Civic and Michael Miklaucic, eds, *Monopoly of Force: The Nexus of DDR and SSR* (Washington DC: NDU Press, 2011), 214.

17 Jeffrey Isima, "Cash Payments in Disarmament, Demobilisation

and Reintegration Programmes in Africa," *Journal of Security Sector Management* 2, 3 (September 2004), 4.

18 Sigrid Willibald, "Does Money Work? Cash Transfers to Ex-Combatants in Disarmament, Demobilization and Reintegration Processes," *Disasters* 30, 3 (2006), 319.

19 Courtney R. Rowe, Eric Wiebelhaus-Braum, and Anne-Tyler Morgan, "The Disarmament, Demobilization, and Reintegration of Former Child Soldiers," in Civic and Miklaucic, eds, *Monopoly of Force: The Nexus of DDR and SSR* (Washington DC: NDU Press, 2011), 144.

20 Hazen, "Understanding 'Reintegration'."

3 DISARMAMENT: THE EPHEMERAL BEGINNING

1 Owen Greene, Duncan Hiscock, and Catherine Flew, "Integration and Co-ordination of DDR and SALW Control Programming: Issues, Experience, and Priorities," Thematic Working Paper 3, DDR and Human Security Project (Centre for International Cooperation and Security, University of Bradford, 2008), 2.

2 Mark Sedra, "New Beginning or Return to Arms? The Disarmament, Demobilization and Reintegration Process in Afghanistan," Afghanistan Research Project, http://ag-afghanistan.de/arg/arp/sedra.pdf (accessed December 22, 2009), 2.

3 The practice and codification of retribution is seen in many cultures. It is an aspect of the Pashtunwali code among the Pashtun communities in Afghanistan and Pakistan. In Melanesian societies of the Pacific, it is described as "payback" (see G. W. Trompf, *Payback: The Logic of Retributions in Melanesian Religions*, Cambridge: Cambridge University Press, 1994).

4 Quoted in David Kilcullen, *The Accidental Guerrilla: Fighting Small Wars in the Midst of a Big One* (Oxford: Oxford University Press, 2009), 76.

5 This impact is very clearly seen in small population, small island societies. See Chapter 3 in Philip Alpers and Conor Twyford, *Small Arms in the Pacific*, Occasional Paper 8 (Geneva: Small Arms Survey, 2003).

6 IDDRS, module 1.10, page 2

7 IDDRS, module 4.10, page 3.

8 Philip Alpers, "Gun-Running: From Arrows to Assault Weapons," in John Henderson and Greg Watson, eds, *Securing a Peaceful Pacific* (Christchurch: Canterbury University Press, 2005), 476.

9 Lenisse L. Edloe, "Best Practices for Successful Disarmament, Demobilization, and Reintegration (DDR)," *New Voices in Public Policy* 1 (Spring 2007), George Mason University School of Public Policy, 11.

10 Alpaslan Özerdem, *Post-War Recovery: Disarmament, Demobilization, and Reintegration* (London and New York: I. B. Tauris, 2009), 27.

11 Berdal, *Disarmament and Demobilisation*, 20.

12 Özerdem, *Post-War Recovery*, 15.

13 United Nations Department of Peacekeeping Operations (UNDPKO), *Disarmament, Demobilization and Reintegration of Ex-Combatants in a Peacekeeping Environment: Principles and Guidelines* (New York: Lessons Learned Unit, United Nations Department of Peacekeeping Operations, 2000), 51.

14 Sedra, "New Beginning or Return to Arms?", 9.

15 Ibid., 9.

16 Peter Dahl Thruelsen, "From Soldier to Civilian: Disarmament, Demobilisation Reintegration in Afghanistan," DIIS Report 7 (Copenhagen: Danish Institute for International Studies, 2006), 25.

17 Ibid., 21–2.

18 Alycia Ebbinghaus, *Getting the Guns off the Ground: Gender and Security Critiques of DDR in Sierra Leone*, Master's thesis (MA thesis, American University, 2007).

19 Stéphanie Pézard, "Sustaining the Conflict: Ammunition for Attack," in Stéphanie Pézard and Holger Anders, eds, *Targeting Ammunition: A Primer* (Geneva: Small Arms Survey, 2006), 135.

20 Alpers, "Gun-Running," 476–7.

21 Pézard, "Sustaining the Conflict," 140.

22 David Capie, *Under the Gun: The Small Arms Challenge in the Pacific* (Wellington: Victoria University Press, 2003), 110.

23 Ibid., 112.

24 Pézard, "Sustaining the Conflict," 148–9.

25 Ibid., 147.
26 Rupert Smith, *The Utility of Force* (New York: Knopf, 2005), 80.
27 Macarten Humphreys and Jeremy M. Weinstein, "Disentangling
    the Determinants of Successful Demobilization and
    Reintegration," Paper Presented at the American Political Science
    Association (Washington, DC, August 2005).
28 Mark Knight and Alpaslan Özerdem, "Guns, Camps and Cash"
    Journal of Peace Research 41, 4 (2004), 505–6.
29 Cate Buchanan and Joaquín Chávez, "Guns and Violence in
    the El Salvador Peace Negotiations," Negotiating Disarmament
    Country Study 3 (Geneva: Centre for Humanitarian Dialogue,
    March 2008), 21.
30 Barnett Rubin, "Identifying Options and Entry Points
    for Disarmament, Demobilization, and Reintegration in
    Afghanistan," www.cic.nyu.edu/peacebuilding/oldpdfs/General_
    DDR_paper2.pdf, March 2003 (accessed March 11, 2010), 6.
31 Sami Faltas, Glenn McDonald, and Camilla Waszink, "Removing
    Small Arms from Society: A Review of Weapons Collection and
    Destruction Programmes" (Geneva: Small Arms Survey, 2001),
    4.
32 In the Australia case, see Wang-Sheng Lee and Sandy Suardi,
    "The Australian Firearms Buyback and Its Effect on Gun
    Deaths," Melbourne Institute Working Paper Series 17/08,
    August 2008.
33 Willibald, "Does Money Work?", 317.
34 Ibid., 331.
35 Joanna Spear, "Disarmament, Demobilization, Reinsertion,
    and Reintegration in Africa," in Oliver Furley and Roy May, eds,
    Ending Africa's Wars: Progressing to Peace (Burlington: Ashgate,
    2006), 64.
36 Knight and Özerdem, "Guns, Camps and Cash," 506.
37 Faltas, McDonald, and Waszink, "Removing Small Arms from
    Society," 3.
38 Buchanan and Chávez, "Guns and Violence," 22.
39 Ibid., 22.
40 Jeremy Ginifer, *Managing Arms in Peace Processes: Rhodesia/
    Zimbabwe* (Geneva: United Nations Institute for Disarmament
    Research, 1995), p. 21.
41 Irena Cristalis, *East Timor: A Nation's Bitter Dawn* (London: Zed
    Books), 171.

42 Audrey Kurth Cronin notes accurately that "terrorism" is a
    pejorative, while being an "insurgent" carries a certain amount
    of credibility. Many terrorist groups hope to evolve into being
    considered an insurgency. See Cronin, *How Terrorism Ends:
    Understanding the Decline and Demise of Terrorist Campaigns*
    (Princeton: Princeton University Press, 2009).

43 Sarah Meek, "Buy or Barter: The History and Prospects of
    Voluntary Weapons Collection Programmes," Monograph 22,
    http://www.iss.co.za/static/templates/tmpl_html.php?node_
    id=489&slink_id=520&slink_type=12&link_id=19 (accessed
    December 22, 2009) (Institute for Security Studies, 1998).

44 Eric Berman, *Managing Arms in Peace Processes: Mozambique*
    (New York: United Nations Institute for Disarmament Research,
    1996), 72.

45 Gwinyayi A. Dzinesa, "Postconflict Disarmament,
    Demobilization, and Reintegration of Former Combatants in
    Southern Africa," *International Studies Perspectives* 8 (2007), 76.

46 Berman, "Managing Arms," 74–5.

47 Faltas, McDonald, and Waszink, "Removing Small Arms from
    Society," 13.

48 Ibid., 14.

49 Muggah, "No Magic Bullet," 247.

50 Ibid., 246.

51 The Bank's Operational Manual states in OP 2.30 "Development
    Cooperation and Conflict, under section 3(a), "Principles of
    Bank Involvement": "In view of its mandate, the Bank does not
    engage in peacemaking or peacekeeping, which are functions
    of the United Nations and certain regional organizations. It
    also does not provide direct support for disarming combatants."
    (January 2001, revised June 2005. http://go.worldbank.org/
    QWWKAOJSW0 (accessed May 12, 2010). In contrast to this
    justification, see Muggah, "No Magic Bullet," 244. Muggah
    argues that the Bank's reluctance to fund disarmament may
    have more to do with the Bank avoiding a risk to its reputation
    in a failed disarmament program rather than a true mandate
    restriction.

52 Dzinesa, "Postconflict Disarmament," 75.

53 Kathleen M. Jennings, "The Struggle to Satisfy: DDR Through
    the Eyes of Ex-Combatants in Liberia," *International Peacekeeping*
    14, 2 (April 2007), 208–9. The initial estimate for combatants

was 38,000. When the disarmament and demobilization phases were declared over in 2004, over 100,000 had disarmed and over 92,000 were considered demobilized. Moreover, just over 27,000 weapons (and some six million rounds of ammunition) were turned in, a ratio of one weapons per every four fighters. This is in stark contrast to the UN Mission's February 2003 estimate of three weapons per combatant.

54 Ibid., 215.
55 Ibid., 211.
56 Nelson Alusala, *Armed Conflict and Disarmament: Selected Central African Case Studies*, ISS Monograph Series no. 129 (March 2007), 2.
57 See generally Charles Fruehling Springwood, ed., *Open Fire: Understanding Global Gun Cultures* (Oxford: Berg, 2007).
58 Quoted in Knight and Özerdem, "Guns, Camps and Cash," 504.
59 Jimmie Briggs, *Innocents Lost: When Child Soldiers Go to War* (New York: Basic Books), 163.
60 Eric Hobsbawm, "Barbarism – A User's Guide," *New Left Review* 1, 206 (July/August 1994), 52.
61 See for example Small Arms Survey, "Gun Culture in Kosovo," in *Small Arms Survey 2005: Weapons at War* (Geneva: Small Arms Survey, 2005). The chapter also cites cases in El Salvador, Georgia, Kyrgyzstan, and Tajikistan. The chapter concludes that accusations of a gun culture are too simplistic and are not based on much empirical research.
62 See Kumar Rupesinghe and Marcial Rubio C., eds, *The Culture of Violence* (Tokyo: United Nations University Press, 1994) for an excellent, overarching review of the concept.
63 South Eastern and Eastern Europe Clearinghouse for the Control of Small Arms and Light Weapons (SEESAC), "The Rifle has the Devil Inside: Gun Culture in South Eastern Europe," Belgrade: SEESAC, 2006, 1.
64 Peter Waldmann, "Is There a Culture of Violence in Colombia?" *International Journal of Conflict and Violence* 1, 1 (2007), 64.
65 Kimberly Theidon, "Reconstructing Masculinities: The Disarmament, Demobilization, and Reintegration of Former Combatants in Colombia," *Human Rights Quarterly* 31, 1 (February 2009), 5.
66 Ibid., 5, emphasis in original.

4 DEMOBILIZATION: THE REAL HEART OF THE
MATTER

1 Berdal, *Disarmament and Destabilisation*, 24.
2 Patricia A. Maulden, *Former Child Soldiers and Sustainable Peace Processes: Demilitarizing the Body, Heart, and Mind* (PhD dissertation, George Mason University, 2007), 111.
3 DPKO 1999, 15.
4 IDDRS, module 1.10, page 2.
5 Alec Campbell, "Where Do All the Soldiers Go? Veterans and the Politics of Demobilization," in Diane E. Davis and Anthony W. Pereira, eds, *Irregular Armed Forces and Their Role in Politics and State Formation* (Cambridge: Cambridge University Press, 2003), 113.
6 Thruelsen, "From Soldier to Civilian," 21.
7 Ibid., 21.
8 Richard Synge, *Mozambique: UN Peacekeeping in Action 1992–94* (Washington, DC: US Institute of Peace Press, 1997), 95.
9 Maulden, *Former Child Soldiers*, 111.
10 Larry J. Woods and Colonel Timothy R. Reese, *Military Interventions in Sierra Leone: Lessons from a Failed State* (Fort Leavenworth: Combat Studies Institute Press Long War Occasional Paper 28, 2008), 17–18.
11 Wolf-Christian Paes, "The Challenges of Disarmament, Demobilization, and Reintegration in Liberia," *International Peacekeeping* 12, 2 (Summer 2005), 255.
12 Ibid., 256.
13 Ibid., 257.
14 Rosellen Roche, "'You Know America Has Drive-By Shootings? In Creggan, We Have Drive-By Beatings.' Continuing Intracommunity Vigilantism in Urban Northern Ireland," in David Pratten and Atreyee Sen, eds, *Global Vigilantes* (New York: Columbia University Press, 2008), 215–18.
15 Jorge A. Restrepo and Robert Muggah, "Colombia's Quiet Demobilization: A Security Dividend?" in Robert Muggah, ed., *Security and Post-Conflict Reconstruction: Dealing with Fighters in the Aftermath of War* (London and New York: Routledge, 2009), 34.
16 Edward Luttwak, "Give War a Chance," *Foreign Policy* (July/ August 1999).

17 Alusala, *Armed Conflict and Disarmament*, 45–6.
18 Berman, *Managing Arms*, 71.
19 Synge, *Mozambique*, 112.
20 Roger Southall, "A Long Prelude to Peace: African Involvement in Ending Burundi's War," in Oliver Furley and Roy May, eds, *Ending Africa's Wars: Progressing to Peace* (Burlington: Ashgate, 2006), 219.
21 See generally Monica Wehner and Donald Denoon, *Without a Gun: Australians' Experience Monitoring Peace in Bougainville 1997–2001* (Canberra: Pandanus Books, 2001).
22 Ginifer, *Managing Arms in Peace Processes*.
23 Bishnu Pathak, "Global Practices of DDR-SSR: Military Services SSR in Nepal," Situation Update 87, Conflict Studies Center, Kathmandu, Nepal (August 29, 2009), 14.
24 United Nations Department of Peacekeeping Operations, *Disarmament, Demobilization and Reintegration*, 36.
25 Knight and Özerdem, "Guns, Camps, and Cash," 508.
26 Ibid.
27 Ibid., 507.
28 Özerdem, *Post-War Recovery*, 19.
29 Kees Kingma, "Demobilization, Reintegration and Peacebuilding in Africa," in Edward Newman and Albrecht Schabel, eds, *Recovering from Civil Conflict: Reconciliation, Peace, and Development* (London: Frank Cass Publishers, 2002), 181.
30 Ibid., 182.
31 Ginifer, *Managing Arms*, 69.
32 Berman, *Managing Arms*.
33 Berdal, *Disarmament and Demobilisation*, 54.
34 Synge, *Mozambique*, 100.
35 Virginia Gamba, "Managing Violence: Disarmament and Demobilization," in John Darby and Roger MacGinty, eds, *Contemporary Peacemaking: Conflict, Violence, and Peace Processes* (New York: Palgrave, 2003), 125.
36 Rocky Williams, *South African Guerrilla Armies: The Impact of Guerrilla Armies on the Creation of South Africa's Armed Forces*, Monograph 127 (Pretoria: Institute for Security Studies, September 2006), 43.
37 Cited in Alpaslan Özerdem, "Insurgency, Militias and DDR as

Part of Security Sector Reconstruction in Iraq: How Not to Do It," *Disasters* 34 (2010), S44.

38 Ibid., S44.

39 Simon Rynn, Owen Green, with Subindra Bogati, *Disarmament, Demobilisation and Reintegration in Nepal*, Mini Case Study, Centre for International Cooperation and Security, Saferworld and University of Bradford (July 2008), 1.

40 Karon Conchran-Budathoki, "Security Sector Reform in Nepal: The Role of Civil Society," http://www.usip.org/publications/security-sector-reform-nepal-role-civil-society (December 2006) (accessed December 30, 2010).

41 Kilcullen, *The Accidental Guerrilla*, 126–7.

42 Codou Bop, " Women in Conflicts: Their Gains and Their Losses," in Sheila Meintjes, Meredith Turshen, and Anu Pillay, eds, *The Aftermath: Women in Post-Conflict Transformation* (London: Zed Books, 2001.

43 Lisa Alfredson, "Child Soldiers, Displacement and Human Security," *Disarmament Forum* 3 (2002), 18.

44 Tunde B. Zack-Williams, "Child Soldiers in Sierra Leone and the Problems of Demobilisation, Rehabilitation and Reintegration into Society: Some Lessons for Social Workers in War-torn Societies," *Social Work Education* 25, 2 (March 2006), 123. Also, see C. J. Chivers, *The Gun* (New York: Simon and Schuster, 2010) for a social history of the development of automatic weapons.

45 Alfredson, "Child Soldiers," 17.

46 Berdal, *Disarmament and Demobilisation*, 54.

47 Synge, *Mozambique*, 109.

48 Philip Verwimp and Marijke Verpoorten, "'What Are All the Soldiers Going to Do?' Demobilisation, Reintegration and Employment in Rwanda," *Conflict, Security and Development* 4, 1 (April 2004), 55.

49 Danny Hoffman, "The Meaning of a Militia: Understanding the Civil Defence Forces of Sierra Leone," *African Affairs* 106, 425 (2007), 639.

50 Ibid., 660.

51 Berdal, *Disarmament and Demobilisation*, 23.

52 Morten Bøås and Anne Hatløy, "'Getting In, Getting Out': Militia Membership and Prospects for Re-Integration in Post-War Liberia," *Journal of Modern African Studies* 46, 1 (2008).

53 Ibid., 38.

5 REINTEGRATION: THE END OF THE BEGINNING

1 IDDRS, module 1.10, page 2.
2 Robert Muggah, "Introduction: The Emperor's Clothes?" in Muggah, ed., *Security and Post-Conflict Reconstruction*, 8.
3 Dmitry Pozhidaev and Ravza Andzhelich, "Beating Swords into Plowshares: Reintegration of Former Combatants in Kosovo," Center for Political and Social Research, Pristina, Kosovo (February 2005), 2.
4 Ibid., 5.
5 IDDRS, module 1.10, page 2.
6 Oliver Furley and Roy May, "Introduction," in Oliver Furley and Roy May, eds, *Ending Africa's Wars: Progressing to Peace* (Burlington, VT: Ashgate, 2006) , 2
7 Pozhidaev and Andzhelich, "Beating Swords," 39.
8 Kathleen Jennings, "The Struggle to Satisfy: DDR through the Eyes of Ex-Combatants in Liberia," *International Peacekeeping* 14, 2 (April 2007), 213–14.
9 Kees Kingma, *Demobilisation in Sub-Saharan Africa* (London: Macmillan, 2000), 46.
10 Gamba, "Managing Violence", 133.
11 Kingma, "Demobilisation, Reintegration, and Peacebuilding," 188.
12 Anthony L. Smith, "Indonesia and the United States 2004–2005: New President, New Needs, Same Old Relations," *The Asia-Pacific and the United States 2004–2005* (Honolulu: Asia-Pacific Center for Security Studies, February 2005), 4. Smith also notes that the December 2004 tsunami created opportunities for US–Indonesia cooperation, including the sale of military equipment to Indonesia for the first time since the Timor separation in 1999. Critically, that weapons sale included the restriction that the weapons could not be used against Aceh rebels.
13 International Crisis Group, "Jihadi Surprise in Aceh," Asia Report 189 (Jakarta and Brussels: International Crisis Group, April 2010), 1.
14 Robert Muggah, "Listening for a Change! Participatory Evaluations of DDR and Arms Reduction in Mali, Colombia and Albania" (Geneva: United Nations Institute for Disarmament Research, 2005), 2.

15 Angela Veale, *From Child Soldier to Ex-Fighter: Female Fighters, Demobilisation, and Reintegration in Ethiopia* (Pretoria: Institute for Security Studies, 2003), 39.
16 Kingma, "Demobilisation, Reintegration, and Peacebuilding in Africa," 196.
17 Özerdem, *Post-War Recovery*, 200.
18 Macarten Humphreys and Jeremy Weinstein, "Demobilization and Reintegration in Sierra Leone: Assessing Progress," in Muggah, ed., *Security and Post-Conflict Reconstruction*, 49.
19 Pozhidaev and Andzhelich, "Beating Swords," 53. See also Hoffman, "The Meaning of a Militia."
20 Besides the Colombia, El Salvador, and Northern Ireland cases mentioned previously, see Dennis Rodgers, "When Vigilantes Turn Bad: Gangs, Violence, and Social Change in Urban Nicaragua," in Pratten and Sen, eds, *Global Vigilantes*.
21 Willibald, "Does Money Work?", 318.
22 Synge, *Mozambique*, 98.
23 Özerdem, *Post-War Recovery*, 64.
24 See ibid., 194–201 for a concise discussion of these issues in the cases of Alfghanistan, El Salvador, Kosovo, and Sierra Leone.
25 Verwimp and Verpoorten, "What Are All the Soldiers Going to Do?", 54.
26 Özerdem, *Post-War Recovery*, 214–15.
27 Mariam Khokhar, *The Dynamics of Demobilizing Under Friendly Governments: The Contras, the Paras, and DDR* (MA thesis, International Peace and Conflict Resolution, American University, 2008).
28 Woods and Reese, *Military Interventions*, 33.
29 Özerdem, *Post-War Recovery*, 192.
30 Kingma, "Demobilization, Reintegration, and Peacebuilding," 189.
31 Lars Waldorf, "Ex-Combatants and Truth Commissions," in Ana Cutter Patel, Pablo De Greiff, and Lars Waldorf, eds, *Disarming the Past: Transitional Justice and Ex-Combatants* (New York: Social Science Research Commission, 2009), 109.
32 Ibid., 112–13. The practice of most Truth Commissions does not include an adversarial cross-examination. It is not meant to be a trial. However, this means that there is little in the structure of the commission that leads to the exposing of false testimony.
33 Cristalis, *East Timor*, 170–1.

34 Kingma, "Demobilization, Reintegration, and Peacebuilding," 192.
35 Zack-Williams, "Child Soldiers in Sierra Leone," 126–7.
36 Briggs, *Innocents Lost*, 32–3.
37 Andrew Rigby, "Civil Society, Reconciliation and Conflict Transformation in Post-War Africa," in Furley and May, eds, *Ending Africa's Wars.*
38 Jon Fraenkel, *The Manipulation of Custom: From Uprising to Intervention in the Solomon Islands* (Wellington: Victoria University Press, 2004), 118
39 Ibid., 110.
40 Ibid., 114.
41 Roger MacGinty, "The Role of Symbols in Peacemaking," in John Darby and Roger MacGinty, eds, *Contemporary Peacekeeping: Conflict, Violence and Peace Processes* (New York: Palgrave Macmillan, 2003), 239
42 This author experienced the excitement and resistance over new symbols on a visit to Kosovo in 2008. While shopping at a market in Pristina, I asked to purchase a Kosovo flag. An older merchant handed me the Albanian flag, saying "This is our flag, we are all Albanians." At the same time, a group of younger individuals (including my interpreter) offered to buy me the Kosovo national flag with visible pride in "their" nation's flag.
43 MacGinty, "The Role of Symbols," 242.
44 Alpaslan Özerdem, "Disarmament, Demobilisation and Reintegration of Former Combatants in Afghanistan: Lessons Learned from a Cross-cultural Perspective," *Third World Quarterly* 23, 5 (2002).

6 CHALLENGES AND CONCLUSIONS

1 Robert Muggah, "Introduction: The Emperor's Clothes?" in Muggah, ed., *Security and Post-Conflict Reconstruction.*
2 Restrepo and Muggah, "Colombia's Quiet Demobilization," 35.
3 Anders Themnér, *Violence in Post-Conflict Societies: Remarginalization, Remobilizers, and Relationships* (London and New York: Routledge, 2011), 148–9.
4 Muggah, "Listening for a Change!", 5.

5 Ibid., 13.
6 Ebbinghaus, *Getting the Guns off the Ground*.
7 Verwimp and Verpoorten, "'What Are All the Soldiers Going to Do?'.
8 Muggah, "The Emperor's Clothes?", 9.
9 Melanne A. Civic and Michael Miklaucic, "Introduction: The State and the Use of Force: Monopoly and Legitimacy," in Civic and Miklaucic, eds, *Monopoly of Force*, xviii–xix.
10 See Paul Shemella, "Interagency Coordination: The Other Side of CIMIC," *Small Wars and Insurgencies* 17, 4 (December 2006).
11 Greene et al., "Integration and Co-ordination of DDR and SALW Control Programming," 4.
12 See Akitoshi Miyashita, "Where Do Norms Come From? Foundations of Japan's Postwar Pacifism," and Yoichiro Sato, "Three Norms of Collective Defense and Japanese Overseas Troop Dispatches," in Yoichiro Sato and Keiko Hirata, eds, *Norms, Interests, and Power in Japanese Foreign Policy* (New York: Palgrave Macmillan, 2008).
13 Özerdem, *Post-War Recovery*, 153.
14 Simon Massey, "Multi-Party Mediation in the Guinea-Bissau Civil War," in Furley and May, eds, *Ending Africa's Wars*, 89–90.
15 Jennings, "The Struggle to Satisfy," 215.
16 Kingma, "Demobilization, Reintegration, and Peacebuilding," 194.
17 This is not to suggest that increased organized criminal activity is never a threat to a country's political stability. See generally Max G. Manwaring, *A Contemporary Challenge to State Sovereignty: Gangs and Other Illicit Transnational Criminal Organizations in Central America, El Salvador, Mexico, Jamaica, and Brazil* (Carlisle: Strategic Studies Institute, December 2007) for a discussion of the political threat offered by what he refers to as "Third Generation Gangs."
18 Dipak K. Gupta, *Understanding Terrorism and Political Violence: The Life Cycle of Birth, Growth, Transformation, and Demise* (New York: Routledge, 2008), 157.
19 Buchanan and Chavez, "Guns and Violence", 20.
20 Berdal, *Disarmament and Demobilisation*, 59.
21 Muggah, "Introduction: The Emperor's Clothes?", 10.

22 Hazen, "Understanding 'Reintegration'."
23 Berdal, *Disarmament and Demobilisation*, 61.
24 Muggah, "Listening for a Change!", 16.
25 David Kilcullen, "Measuring Progress in Afghanistan," humanterrainsystem.army.mil/.../Measuring%20Progress%20 Afghanistan%20(2).pdf (accessed March 30, 2011), 18.
26 Richard Jackson, "Africa's Wars: Overview, Causes, and Challenges of Conflict Transformation," in Furley and May, eds, *Ending Africa's Wars*, 26, emphasis added.

Bibliography

Alden, Chris, Monika Thakur, and Matthew Arnold, *Militias and the Challenges of Post-Conflict Peace: Silencing the Guns* (London: Zed Books, 2011).

Alfredson, Lisa, "Child Soldiers, Displacement and Human Security," *Disarmament Forum* 3 (2002).

Alpers, Philip, "Gun-Running: From Arrows to Assault Weapons," in John Henderson and Greg Watson, eds, *Securing a Peaceful Pacific* (Christchurch: Canterbury University Press, 2005).

Alpers, Philip, and Conor Twyford, *Small Arms in the Pacific*, Occasional Paper 8 (Geneva: Small Arms Survey, 2003).

Alusala, Nelson, *Armed Conflict and Disarmament: Selected Central African Case Studies*, ISS Monograph Series no. 129 (March 2007).

Berdal, Mats R., *Disarmament and Demobilisation after Civil Wars*, Adelphi Paper 303 (Oxford: International Institute for Strategic Studies, 1996).

Berman, Eric, *Managing Arms in Peace Processes Mozambique* (New York: United Nations Institutute for Disarmament Research, 1996).

Bishop, Patrick, *Ground Truth* (London: HarperPress, 2009)

Bøås Morten, and Anne Hatløy, "'Getting In, Getting Out': Militia Membership and Prospects for Re-Integration in Post-War Liberia," *Journal of Modern African Studies* 46, 1 (2008).

Bop, Codou, " Women in Conflicts: Their Gains and Their Losses," in Sheila Meintjes, Meredith Turshen, and Anu Pillay, eds, *The Aftermath: Women in Post-Conflict Transformation* (London: Zed Books), 2001.

Boshoff, Henri, "The Demobilisation, Disarmament, and Reintegration Process in the Democratic Republic of the Congo. A Never-Ending Story!" Institute for Security Studies Situation Report (2 July 2007).

Briggs, Jimmie, *Innocents Lost: When Child Soldiers Go to War* (New York: Basic Books 2005).

Buchanan, Cate, and Joaquín Chávez, "Guns and Violence in the El Salvador Peace Negotiations," Negotiating Disarmament Country Study 3 (Geneva: Centre for Humanitarian Dialogue, March 2008).

Campbell, Alec, "Where Do All the Soldiers Go? Veterans and the Politics of Demobilization," in Diane E. Davis and Anthony W. Pereira, eds, *Irregular Armed Forces and Their Role in Politics and State Formation* (Cambridge: Cambridge University Press, 2003).

Capie, David, *Under the Gun: The Small Arms Challenge in the Pacific* (Christchurch: Victoria University Press, 2003).

Chivers, C. J., *The Gun* (New York: Simon and Schuster, 2010).

Civic, Melanne A., and Michael Miklaucic, eds, *Monopoly of Force: The Nexus of DDR and SSR* (Washington, DC: NDU Press, 2011).

Cohen, Jared, *Children of Jihad: A Young American's Travels Among the Youth of the Middle East* (New York: Gotham Books, 2007).

Conchran-Budathoki, Karon, "Security Sector Reform in Nepal: The Role of Civil Society," http://www.usip.org/publications/security-sector-reform-nepal-role-civil-society (December 2006) (accessed December 30, 2010).

Cristalis, Irena, *East Timor: A Nation's Bitter Dawn* (London: Zed Books, 2009).

Cronin, Audrey Kurth, *How Terrorism Ends: Understanding the Decline and Demise of Terrorist Campaigns* (Princeton: Princeton University Press, 2009).

Douglas, Ian, Colin Gleichmann, Michael Odenwald, Kees Steenken, and Adrian Wilkinson, *Disarmament, Demobilisation, and Reintegration: A Practical Field and Classroom Guide* (Frankfurt: Druckerei Hassmüller Graphische Betriebe GmbH and Co., 2004).

Dudouet, Véronique, "Nonstate Armed Groups and the Politics of Postwar Security Governance," in Melanne A. Civic and Michael Miklaucic, eds, *Monopoly of Force: The Nexus of DDR and SSR* (Washington, DC: NDU Press, 2011).

Dzinesa, Gwinyayi A., "Postconflict Disarmament, Demobilization, and Reintegration of Former Combatants in Southern Africa," *International Studies Perspectives* 8 (2007).

Ebbinghaus, Alycia, *Getting the Guns off the Ground: Gender and Security Critiques of DDR in Sierra Leone* (MA thesis, International Relations, American University, 2007).

Edloe, Lenisse L., "Best Practices for Successful Disarmament, Demobilization, and Reintegration (DDR)," *New Voices in Public Policy* 1 (Spring 2007).

Faltas, Sami, Glenn McDonald, and Camilla Waszink, *Removing Small Arms from Society: A Review of Weapons Collection and Destruction Programmes* (Geneva: Small Arms Survey, 2001).

Fraenkel, Jon, *The Manipulation of Custom: From Uprising to Intervention in the Solomon Islands* (Wellington: Victoria University Press, 2004).

Francis, David J., "Introduction," *Civil Militia: Africa's Intractable Security Menace?* (Burlington, VT: Ashgate, 2005).

Furley, Oliver and Roy May, "Introduction," in Oliver Furley and Roy May, eds, *Ending Africa's Wars: Progressing to Peace* (Burlington, VT: Ashgate, 2006).

Gamba, Virginia, "Managing Violence: Disarmament and Demobilization," in John Darby and Roger MacGinty, eds, *Contemporary Peacemaking: Conflict, Violence and Peace Processes* (New York: Palgrave MacMillan, 2003).

Gentile, Gian, "Let's Build an Army to Win *All* Wars," *Joint Forces Quarterly* 52, 1 (2009): 27–33.

Ginifer, Jeremy, *Managing Arms in Peace Processes: Rhodesia/Zimbabwe* (New York: United Nations, 1995).

Greene, Owen, Duncan Hiscock, and Catherine Flew, "Integration and Co-ordination of DDR and SALW Control Programming: Issues, Experience, and Priorities," Thematic Working Paper 3, DDR and Human Security Project (Centre for International Cooperation and Security, University of Bradford, 2008).

Gupta, Dipak K., *Understanding Terrorism and Political Violence: The Life Cycle of Birth, Growth, Transformation, and Demise* (New York: Routledge, 2008).

Hazen, Jennifer M., "Understanding 'Reintegration' within Postconflict Peacebuilding: Making the Case for 'Reinsertion' First and Better Linkages Thereafter," in Melanne A. Civic and Michael Miklaucic, eds, *Monopoly of Force: The Nexus of DDR and SSR* (Washington, DC: NDU Press, 2011).

Headquarters, Department of the Army, *Counterinsurgency* FM 3–24 (Washington, DC: Headquarters, Department of the Army, 2006).

Hobsbawm, Eric, "Barbarism – A User's Guide," *New Left Review* 1, 206 (July/August 1994).

Hoffman, Danny, "The Meaning of a Militia: Understanding the Civil Defence Forces of Sierra Leone," *African Affairs* 106, 425 (2007).

Humphreys, Macarten, and Jeremy Weinstein, "Demobilization and Reintegration in Sierra Leone: Assessing Progress," in Robert Muggah, ed., *Security and Post-Conflict Reconstruction: Dealing with*

Fighters in the Aftermath of War (London and New York: Routledge, 2009).

Humphreys, Macarten, and Jeremy M. Weinstein, "Disentangling the Determinants of Successful Demobilization and Reintegration," Paper Presented at the American Political Science Association (Washington, DC, August 2005).

Iklé, Fred Charles, *Every War Must End*, Second Edition, Revised (New York: Columbia University Press, 2005).

International Crisis Group, "Jihadi Surprise in Aceh," Asia Report 189 (Jakarta and Brussels: International Crisis Group, April 2010).

Isima, Jeffrey, "Cash Payments in Disarmament, Demobilisation and Reintegration Programmes in Africa," *Journal of Security Sector Management* 2, 3 (September 2004).

Jackson, Richard, "Africa's Wars: Overview, Causes, and Challenges of Conflict Transformation," in Oliver Furley and Roy May, eds, *Ending Africa's Wars: Progressing to Peace* (Burlington, VT: Ashgate, 2006).

Jennings, Kathleen M., "The Struggle to Satisfy: DDR Through the Eyes of Ex-Combatants in Liberia," *International Peacekeeping* 14, 2 (April 2007).

Johnson, Wray, "Doctrine for Irregular Warfare: Déjà Vu All Over Again?" *Marine Corps University Journal* 2, 1 (Spring 2011).

Keen, David, *Conflict and Collusion in Sierra Leone* (Oxford: James Surrey, 2005).

Khokhar, Mariam, *The Dynamics of Demobilizing Under Friendly Governments: The Contras The Paras, and DDR* (MA thesis, International Peace and Conflict Resolution, American University, 2008).

Kilcullen, David, *The Accidental Guerrilla: Fighting Small Wars in the Midst of a Big One* (Oxford: Oxford University Press, 2009).

Kilcullen, David, "Measuring Progress in Afghanistan," humanterrainsystem.army.mil/.../Measuring%20Progress%20Afghanistan%20 (2).pdf (accessed March 30, 2011).

Kingma, Kees, *Demobilisation in Sub-Saharan Africa* (London: Macmillan, 2000).

Kingma, Kees, "Demobilization, Reintegration and Peacebuilding in Africa," in Edward Newman and Albrecht Schabel, eds, *Recovering from Civil Conflict: Reconciliation, Peace, and Development* (London: Frank Cass Publishers, 2002).

Knight, Mark, "Expanding the DDR Model: Politics and Organisations," *Journal of Security Sector Management* 6, 1 (March 2008).

Knight, Mark, and Alpaslan Özerdem, "Guns, Camps and Cash," *Journal of Peace Research* 41, 4 (July 2004).

Luttwak, Edward, "Give War a Chance," *Foreign Policy* (July/August 1999).

MacGinty, Roger, "The Role of Symbols in Peacemaking," in John Darby and Roger MacGinty, eds, *Contemporary Peacekeeping: Conflict, Violence and Peace Processes* (New York: Palgrave MacMillan, 2003).

Manwaring, Max G., *A Contemporary Challenge to State Sovereignty: Gangs and Other Illicit Transnational Criminal Organizations in Central America, El Salvador, Mexico, Jamaica, and Brazil* (Carlisle: Strategic Studies Institute, 2007).

Manwaring, Max G., *Urban Gangs: The New Insurgency* (Carlisle Barracks: Strategic Studies Institute, 2005).

Marriage, Zoë, "Flip-Flop Rebel, Dollar Soldier: Demobilisation in the Democratic Republic of Congo," *Conflict, Security, and Development* 7, 2 (June 2007).

Massey, Simon, "Multi-Party Mediation in the Guinea-Bissau Civil War," in Oliver Furley and Roy May, eds, *Ending Africa's Wars: Progressing to Peace* (Burlington, VT: Ashgate, 2006).

Maulden, Patricia A., *Former Child Soldiers and Sustainable Peace Processes: Demilitarizing the Body, Heart, and Mind* (PhD Dissertation, George Mason University, 2007).

McFate, Sean, "There's a New Sheriff in Town: DDR-SSR and the Monopoly of Force," in Melanne A. Civic and Michael Miklaucic, eds, *Monopoly of Force: The Nexus of DDR and SSR* (Washington, DC: NDU Press, 2011).

Meek, Sarah, "Buy or Barter: The History and Prospects of Voluntary Weapons Collection Programmes," Monograph 22, http://www.iss.co.za/static/templates/tmpl_html.php?node_id=489&slink_id=520&slink_type=12&link_id=19 (Pretoria: Institute for Security Studies, 1998) (accessed December 22, 2009).

Miyashita, Akitoshi, "Where Do Norms Come From? Foundations of Japan's Postwar Pacifism," in Yoichiro Sato and Keiko Hirata, eds, *Norms, Interests, and Power in Japanese Foreign Policy* (New York: Palgrave Macmillan, 2008).

Muggah, Robert, "Introduction: The Emperor's Clothes?", in Robert Muggah, ed., *Security and Post-Conflict Reconstruction: Dealing with Fighters in the Aftermath of War* (London and New York: Routledge, 2009).

Muggah, Robert, "Listening for a Change! Participatory Evaluations of

DDR and Arms Reduction in Mali, Colombia and Albania" (Geneva: United Nations Institute for Disarmament Research, 2005).

Muggah, Robert, "No Magic Bullet: A Critical Perspective on Disarmament, Demobilization and Reintegration (DDR) and Weapons Reduction in Post-conflict Contexts" *The Round Table* 94 (April 2005).

Özerdem, Alpaslan, "Disarmament, Demobilisation and Reintegration of Former Combatants in Afghanistan: Lessons Learned from a Cross-Cultural Perspective," *Third World Quarterly* 23, 5 (2002).

Özerdem, Alpaslan, "Insurgency, Militias and DDR as Part of Security Sector Reconstruction in Iraq: How Not to Do It," *Disasters* 34 (2010).

Özerdem, Alpaslan, *Post-War Recovery: Disarmament, Demobilization, and Reintegration* (London and New York: I. B. Tauris, 2009).

Paes, Wolf-Christian, "The Challenges of Disarmament, Demobilization, and Reintegration in Liberia," *International Peacekeeping* 12, 2 (Summer 2005).

Pathak, Bishnu, "Global Practices of DDR-SSR: Military Services SSR in Nepal," Situation Update 87, Conflict Studies Center, Kathmandu, Nepal (August 29, 2009).

Pézard, Stéphanie, "Sustaining the Conflict: Ammunition for Attack," in Stéphanie Pézard and Holger Anders, eds, *Targeting Ammunition: A Primer* (Geneva: Small Arms Survey, 2006).

Pozhidaev, Dmitry, and Ravza Andzhelich, "Beating Swords into Plowshares: Reintegration of Former Combatants in Kosovo," Center for Political and Social Research, Pristina, Kosovo (February 2005).

Restrepo, Jorge A. and Robert Muggah, "Colombia's Quiet Demobilization: A Security Dividend?" in Robert Muggah, ed., *Security and Post-Conflict Reconstruction: Dealing with Fighters in the Aftermath of War* (London and New York: Routledge, 2009).

Rigby, Andrew, "Civil Society, Reconciliation and Conflict Transformation in Post-War Africa," in Oliver Furley and Roy May, eds, *Ending Africa's Wars: Progressing to Peace* (Burlington, VT: Ashgate, 2006).

Roche, Rosellen, "'You Know America Has Drive-By Shootings? In Creggan, We Have Drive-By Beatings.' Continuing Intracommunity Vigilantism in Urban Northern Ireland," in David Pratten and Atreyee Sen, eds, *Global Vigilantes* (New York: Columbia University Press, 2008).

Rodgers, Dennis, "When Vigilantes Turn Bad: Gangs, Violence, and

Social Change in Urban Nicaragua," in David Pratten and Atreyee Sen, eds, *Global Vigilantes* (New York: Columbia University Press, 2008).

Rowe, Courtney R., Eric Wiebelhaus-Braum, and Anne-Tyler Morgan, "The Disarmament, Demobilization, and Reintegration of Former Child Soldiers," in Melanne A. Civic and Michael Miklaucic, eds, *Monopoly of Force: The Nexus of DDR and SSR* (Washington, DC: NDU Press, 2011).

Rubin, Barnett, "Identifying Options and Entry Points for Disarmament, Demobilization, and Reintegration in Afghanistan," www.cic.nyu.edu/peacebuilding/oldpdfs/General_DDR_paper2.pdf, March 2003 (accessed March 11, 2010).

Rupesinghe, Kumar, and Marcial Rubio C., eds, *The Culture of Violence* (Tokyo: United Nations University Press, 1994).

Rynn, Simon, Owen Greene, with Subindra Bogati, *Disarmament, Demobilisation and Reintegration in Nepal*, Mini Case Study, Centre for International Cooperation and Security, Saferworld and University of Bradford (July 2008).

Sato, Yoichiro, "Three Norms of Collective Defense and Japanese Overseas Troop Dispatches," in Yoichiro Sato and Keiko Hirata, eds, *Norms, Interests, and Power in Japanese Foreign Policy* (New York: Palgrave Macmillan, 2008).

Sato, Yoichiro, and Keiko Hirata eds, *Norms, Interests, and Power in Japanese Foreign Policy* (New York: Palgrave Macmillan, 2008).

Sedra, Mark, "New Beginning or Return to Arms? The Disarmament, Demobilization and Reintegration Process in Afghanistan," Afghanistan Research Project, http://ag-afghanistan.de/arg/arp/sedra.pdf (2003) (accessed December 22, 2009).

Sen, Atreyee and David Pratten, "Global Vigilantes: Perspectives on Justice and Violence," in David Pratten and Atreyee Sen, eds, *Global Vigilantes* (New York: Columbia University Press, 2008).

Shemella, Paul, "Interagency Coordination: The Other Side of CIMIC," *Small Wars and Insurgencies* 17, 4 (December 2006).

Small Arms Survey, "Gun Culture in Kosovo," in *Small Arms Survey 2005: Weapons at War* (Geneva: Small Arms Survey, 2005).

Smith, Anthony L., "Indonesia and the United States 2004–2005: New President, New Needs, Same Old Relations," *The Asia-Pacific and the United States 2004–2005* (Honolulu: Asia-Pacific Center for Security Studies, February 2005).

Smith, Rupert, *The Utility of Force* (New York: Knopf, 2005).

Southall, Roger, "A Long Prelude to Peace: African Involvement in Ending Burundi's War," in Oliver Furley and Roy May, eds, *Ending Africa's Wars: Progressing to Peace* (Burlington, VT: Ashgate, 2006).

South Eastern and Eastern Europe Clearinghouse for the Control of Small Arms and Light Weapons (SEESAC), "The Rifle has the Devil Inside: Gun Culture in South Eastern Europe" (Belgrade: SEESAC, 2006).

Spear, Joanna, "Disarmament, Demobilization, Reinsertion, and Reintegration in Africa," in Oliver Furley and Roy May, eds, *Ending Africa's Wars: Progressing to Peace* (Burlington, VT: Ashgate, 2006).

Springwood, Charles Fruehling, ed., *Open Fire: Understanding Global Gun Cultures* (Oxford: Berg, 2007).

Synge, Richard, *Mozambique: UN Peacekeeping in Action 1992–94* (Washington, DC: US Institute of Peace Press, 1997).

Theidon, Kimberly, "Reconstructing Masculinities: The Disarmament, Demobilization, and Reintegration of Former Combatants in Colombia," *Human Rights Quarterly* 31, 1 (February 2009).

Themnér, Anders, *Violence in Post-Conflict Societies: Remarginalization, Remobilizers, and Relationships* (London and New York: Routledge, 2011).

Thruelsen, Peter Dahl, "From Soldier to Civilian: Disarmament, Demobilisation Reintegration in Afghanistan," DIIS Report 7 (Copenhagen: Danish Institute for International Studies, 2006).

Trompf, G. W., *Payback: The Logic of Retributions in Melanesian Religions* (Cambridge: Cambridge University Press, 1994).

United Nations, *Integrated Disarmament, Demobilization and Reintegration Standards* (IDDRS) (New York: United Nations, 2006).

United Nations Department of Peacekeeping Operations (UNDPKO), *Disarmament, Demobilization and Reintegration of Ex-Combatants in a Peacekeeping Environment: Principles and Guidelines* (New York: Lessons Learned Unit, United Nations Department of Peacekeeping Operations, 2000).

Veale, Angela, *From Child Soldier to Ex-Fighter: Female Fighters, Demobilisation, and Reintegration in Ethiopia* (Pretoria: Institute for Security Studies, 2003).

Verwimp, Philip, and Marijke Verpoorten, "'What Are All the Soldiers Going to Do?' Demobilisation, Reintegration and Employment in Rwanda," *Conflict, Security and Development* 4, 1 (April 2004).

Waldmann, Peter, "Is There a Culture of Violence in Colombia?" *International Journal of Conflict and Violence* 1, 1 (2007).

Waldorf, Lars, "Ex-Combatants and Truth Commissions," in Ana Cutter Patel, Pablo De Greiff, and Lars Waldorf, eds, *Disarming the Past: Transitional Justice and Ex-Combatants* (New York: Social Science Research Commission, 2009).

Wang-Sheng Lee and Sandy Suardi, "The Australian Firearms Buyback and Its Effect on Gun Deaths," Melbourne Institute Working Paper Series 17/08 (August 2008).

Wehner, Monica, and Donald Denoon, *Without a Gun: Australians' Experience Monitoring Peace in Bougainville 1997–2001* (Canberra: Pandanus Books, 2001).

Williams, Phil, *Criminals, Militias, and Insurgents: Organized Crime in Iraq* (Carlisle: Strategic Studies Institute, 2009).

Williams, Rocky, *South African Guerrilla Armies: The Impact of Guerrilla Armies on the Creation of South Africa's Armed Forces*, Monograph 127 (Pretoria: Institute for Security Studies, September 2006).

Willibald, Sigrid, "Does Money Work? Cash Transfers to Ex-Combatants in Disarmament, Demobilization and Reintegration processes," *Disasters* 30, 3 (2006).

Woods, Larry J., and Colonel Timothy R. Reese, *Military Interventions in Sierra Leone: Lessons from a Failed State*, Long War Occasional Paper 28 (Fort Leavenworth: Combat Studies Institute Press, 2008).

World Bank, World Bank Operational Manual, http://go.worldbank.org/QWWKAOJSW0 (January 2001, revised June 2005) (accessed May 12, 2010).

Zack-Williams, Tunde B., "Child Soldiers in Sierra Leone and the Problems of Demobilisation, Rehabilitation and Reintegration into Society: Some Lessons for Social Workers in War-torn Societies," *Social Work Education* 25, 2 (March 2006).

Index